Wing Co

Dizzy Allen

DFC

Fighter Squadron

A Memoir
1940–1942

A MAYFLOWER BOOK

GRANADA
London Toronto Sydney New York

Published by Granada Publishing Limited in 1982

ISBN 0 583 13416 5

First published in Great Britain by
William Kimber & Co. Limited 1979
Copyright © Wing Commander H. R. Allen 1979

Granada Publishing Limited
Frogmore, St Albans, Herts AL2 2NF
and
36 Golden Square, London W1R 4AH
866 United Nations Plaza, New York, NY 10017, USA
117 York Street, Sydney, NSW 2000, Australia
100 Skyway Avenue, Rexdale, Ontario, M9W 3A6, Canada
61 Beach Road, Auckland, New Zealand

Printed and bound in Great Britain
by Cox and Wyman Ltd, Reading
Set in Times

Granada ®
Granada Publishing ®

Contents

List of illustrations

Dedicated to
Rupert Leigh,
My First Squadron Commander,
My Mentor, and My Very Good Friend
For Nearly Forty Years.

Now all the youth of England are on fire,
And silken dalliance in the wardrobe lies.

SHAKESPEARE, *King Henry V*

Preface

I decided that I should become a fighter pilot when I was ten, which probably came about after I read a book on the exploits of Captain Albert Ball, VC, DSO, MC, Royal Flying Corps. In retrospect that was a fairly stupid notion. One could learn to fly only in the Royal Air Force and certain academic prowess would be essential, but at the age of ten I was almost totally uneducated. Furthermore, even if I did manage to get my pilot's brevet in the far future, who could say that I would be selected to join Fighter Command? The bomber was the vogue at that time, and even flying boats were being considered as weapons of war, which meant that my dream might never come to fruition. But hope is as cheap as despair, I believe.

I passed my exams at school and went on to university where I spent most of my time playing tennis or table tennis. I was supposed to be reading Economics, German, Statistics, Commercial French and all things east or west. In fact I was merely biding my time until I was old enough to apply for a commission in the RAF. As age crept up on me I made my application to the Air Ministry. They replied in short time and invited me to be interviewed by a Commissioning Board. My father kindly lent me his car, and shortly afterwards wished he hadn't. I was wearing my best suit, of course. This was 1938, at the time of the Munich 'Agreement' and even I smelled a rat about that. The commissionaire ushered me to the reception desk at Adastral House, and a woman asked me to sign a chit to gain access to the corridors of power. I was thereupon escorted to a waiting-room on the fourth floor.

They kept me waiting as is their wont. Eventually a head poked through the doorway and invited me to face the Board which I did. The members of the Board were all wearing plain clothes, but it was clear that the man in the middle behind the table was the boss, so I called him 'Sir'. The remaining members of the Board were either anonymous or nonentities – to my young eyes at least. One was an earnest, bespectacled mathematician, and when his turn came he asked me:

'Can you multiply in your head $11 \times 23 \times 68$?'

'No,' I replied. 'Can you?'

They passed me as suitable to be given the King's commission in the RAF and told me to go over the road from Adastral House to see the medical wallahs. My reflexes, heart, lungs, blood pressure and so on were checked out, the oculist found I was just a bit short-sighted but not sufficiently to be rejected and then the man with the whirligig took control.

'Sit in this centrifugal chair,' he sternly instructed. 'I will start you off at one Gee and gradually increase the speed to four-and-a-half Gee.'

I didn't know what Gee meant.

Round and round it went with me aboard, gradually increasing its impetus until the blood began to drain from my brain and I blacked out. When I came to, the doctor muttered something to me, whereupon I rose from the chair and promptly fell flat on my face, my head still spinning like a top.

'I didn't ask you to get off the chair, you silly ass,' the doctor said. 'I merely asked you to focus your eyes on my finger so I could gauge your recovery time.'

'In which case,' I replied, 'you should have been more explicit.'

'I'll pass you for the Gee test anyway,' he said. 'Not many people can rise to their feet immediately after having had four-and-a-half Gee applied.'

By nature I have always been more than somewhat impatient, so I fumed while awaiting the formal Air Ministry decree accepting me as an embryo RAF officer. It never occurred to me, of course, that the personnel staff had to plan the intakes into the various *ab initio* training schools. The weeks dragged by, and then I received a bulky buff envelope through the post. With tremulous fingers I tore it open and searched through the pamphlets for the all-important letter.

'Sir', it began, and nobody had ever called me 'Sir' before.

I am instructed to inform you that you have been accepted as a pupil-pilot by the Air Ministry with a view to your being commissioned in the Royal Air Force. I must inform you that a prerequisite to your being granted a commission is that you fly your *ab initio* training aeroplane solo within ten hours' flying under the hands of an instructor.

Enclosed are various pamphlets which we suggest you read. [Little did he know that I had already read the lot.] You are to attend the pupil-pilots' flying training school at Scone Airport, Perth, on 4 June 1939. You are to arrange that your baggage contains . . . [which included a flat cap, not that I had ever worn a flat cap before]. Also enclosed is a railway warrant to take you from Euston Station to Perth where motor transport will be waiting to take you to Scone Airport. You will inform the receptionist at the pupil-pilots' mess of your arrival.

Please acknowledge receipt of this letter and confirm that you are still willing to take up flying training under the aegis of the Air Ministry.

I have the honour to be,
   Sir,
      Your obedient Servant.
      Signed: Archibald Biggs.

So I was in for the preliminary canter, whereupon the first thing I did was to drive to the nearest commercial flying school where I took my first passenger flight. It was in a Tiger Moth, the De Havilland 82, and the pilot merely gave me a circuit and bump and charged me five shillings for the privilege, but at least I had seen the landscape without my feet touching the ground. Next I went shopping to purchase a flat cap, and other things like PT kit.

My parents, especially my mother, distinctly disapproved of my plan to become a pilot in the RAF. She thought I might kill myself, and she was pretty certain I had, after receiving three signals from the Air Ministry within a year or so, posting me as 'missing, believed killed'. I didn't inform her of another fifteen occasions when I was all but killed through enemy action or flying accidents. However, my parents decided to drive me to Perth since they felt in need of a holiday, so I didn't require the Air Ministry railway warrant. We took a slow drive to Perth stopping en route at various hotels, and on arrival I looked for a bed and breakfast house recommended on the list given me by the Air Ministry. It was good enough, the one I found, and my landlady was not only most kind but she gave one a good breakfast as I was to discover. I bade my father and mother as reluctant a farewell as they did to me, and they drove away on a southerly heading while I sorted myself out.

The airfield was about a mile away from my digs, an easy walk, but I decided to call for a taxi. I have always had a sense of the theatrical. I wore my flat cap as, apparently, that was a *sine qua non*, and a security guard called my driver to a halt while he was on the point of entering the precincts of the airport. The security guard was a frail old man who would have been murdered had he even met a small mongrel. He asked me for my name and I handed him the identity card issued by the Air Ministry. He checked it out with the list contained in his hut, agreed I was who I said I was, and informed me that I was the last pupil-pilot to join the course.

'Y'ever flown before?' he inquired.

'No I haven't.'

'Och, there's no problem. Flying is easy, no more difficult than riding a mo'bike.'

'Have you done much flying?' I asked, face alight with innocence.

'Och away. I'm no the man to boast, but I did shoot down twenty enemy aircraft in the war when attached to Richthofen's Circus.'

'But I thought he was German.'

'Nay. That was the other Richthofen.'

I later discovered that he had never flown an aircraft in his life.

Joining a new officers' mess, and I have joined hundreds, was always a traumatic experience – not that the mess at Scone was an officers' mess because we were civilians employed under probation by the Air Ministry for which they paid us the princely sum of twelve shillings and sixpence a week. But it was a similar experience. The receptionist at Scone ticked his book which gave me access to the mess; I already had private rooms down the road, but he assured me that I would be given a room in the mess within a week or so. I entered the anteroom where I found twenty or so men, ages ranging from about nineteen to twenty-six. There were obvious thieves and rogues in the ensemble, but there were also youths of high calibre. The rogues had 'joined' the RAF to keep away from the police, but the others joined for similar reasons to my own. I picked up a newspaper from the large table in the middle of the room which was scattered with newspapers and magazines, sat myself on an armchair in the corner, and covertly kept glancing from behind the newspaper in an attempt to differentiate between the thieves and the gents. My appreciation was about right, but I failed to evaluate a con-man who, ten years later, saw me in Piccadilly and made the fruitless attempt to touch me for a loan of £10.

However, when I was given a room a week later, I bade my landlady a fond farewell and took a taxi brimful of my baggage to Scone. From then on some of the other pupil-pilots and I became a bunch of buddies. We were going to share almost identical experiences and either fail, or falter, or pass into the RAF proper. I swiftly made friends with the gents and kept the rogues at bay.

It was all very interesting; and that kind of existence remained interesting for a quarter of a century and more.

1

Pupil-Pilot

The course formed up as per Daily Orders the next day after
my arrival in the shack wherein we rested, where our flying
clothing lockers were and where the flying instructors had
their various offices. We had already attended the
equipment store and been issued with flying clothes, helmets
with the Gosport tube ready to be plugged in and so forth;
also been measured for our parachutes. The Gosport tube
allowed the trainee pilot to hear his flying instructor as he
shouted into his mask, the sound being relayed through a
series of narrow pipes into the pupil's earpieces on his flying
helmet. Previous to this invention, the instructor had no
recourse other than to tap the pupil on the shoulder from the
rear seat, and make menacing signals if he found fault. The
Gosport system was not entirely reliable, but it was certainly
an improvement on hand signals. The pupil could not reply
to the instructor, only give him the thumbs-up signal if he
comprehended – or imagined he comprehended – the oral
instructions.

I was looking out of the window and saw the flying
instructors arrive, park their cars and disembark. The last of
them all was a man with a flash sports car, two white bull-
terriers, a clipped moustache and a Roman nose. He wore an
RAF blazer, was dapper, erect and looked to me to be a good
guy. He was, as I discovered, the Chief Flying Instructor, a
wizard acrobatic pilot, had taken a short-service commission in the RAF, had been awarded the Air Force Cross for
his gallantry 'not in the face of the enemy', and had left the
RAF to take up a position as a flying instructor with
Airwork Ltd who were contracted by the Air Ministry to
train *ab initio* pilots.

When the instructors had settled down, each member of

the course was ushered into the main office in turn to be sur-
veyed, adjudged and considered with considerable suspicion. I
was the second member of the course to appear before
the Almighty, since my name begins with an 'A'; there was a
man named Alcon who beat me to the post. When I was
called into the interviewing-room, behind the table was a
fearsome gang of men who glared at me, and Flight
Lieutenant Carr was seated in the middle of the Board. He
questioned my credentials and then the others had a go at
me. It was all very civilized, but I knew they were assessing
me very sharply, and trying to discover whether I was a
natural pilot or not. (When you know enough about it this is
an easy decision to take, funnily enough, even on the ground,
as I was to discover over the years.)

Carr told me I would be hearing from him later, and asked
me to leave. Then they continued to interview the other
members of the course. Later that morning after the
processes had been undergone an instructor pinned a piece
of paper on the board in the hut. I glanced at it and noted
that my flying instructor was to be Flight Lieutenant Carr
and that I was his only pupil. I thought that he had seen in me
an embryo Albert Ball and wanted to personally groom me
for stardom. In fact he just shut his eyes and stuck a pin in the
list of pupil-pilots and it happened to land on my name. He
could take only one student for he had to flight-test the
instructors every so often, and perform Chief Flying
Instructor tests on the rest of the pupils. Nevertheless it was a
lucky chance for me because he was a top-grade flying
instructor and a nice person to boot. The other instructors
had four pupils apiece.

Before lunch he came along and told me he would be
showing me how to start the Tiger Moth with which the
Elementary Flying Training School was equipped. He made
sure the magneto switches were off and that the chocks were
firmly in position. Then he demonstrated how the propeller
should be swung in such a way that it wouldn't cut my head
off if I did it wrong. The essential trick was with a right-

handed pilot to take the weight off the right foot at the moment of swinging the airscrew. The jerk made one sway backwards away from the propeller as the engine sparked. The patter had to be very firmly complied with – more than one pilot has lost his hand in this process and more than one has had his head removed neater than Madame Guillotine could ever have achieved it. The patter went like this:

'Petrol on. Switches off. Suck in.'

A couple of pulls of the prop would thereby ensure that the carburettors were filled. The next command was:

'Ready to start. Petrol on. Switches on. Contact!'

Then, given a stroke of luck, a hefty pull on the airscrew would set the engine running.

The theory was that a pilot had to know how to start his engine without the aid of mechanics if he forced-landed in a field. This was nonsense, for we didn't carry chocks in the Tiger Moth, and if an attempt had been made to get the engine running without them, the aeroplane, having no brakes, would begin to roll and chase the pilot the length and breadth of the meadow. More apposite was the fact that provided the pilot knew the drill then he wouldn't decapitate his mechanic.

Anyway I started the engine to his satisfaction and then he gave me a lift to the mess in his Frazer-Nash together with his two big bull-terriers.

The sequence of flying training as an *ab initio* pilot was as follows:

1. Air experience for pupil.
2. Effect of controls.
3. Taxi-ing and handling of engine.
4. Straight and level flying.
5. Stalling, climbing and gliding.
6. Medium turns with and without engine.
7. Taking off into wind.
8. Approaches and landings.

9. Preliminary action in the event of fire including stopping and starting engine.
10. Spinning.
11. First solo.
12. Side-slipping
13. Further action in the event of fire.
14. Low flying (with instructor only).
15. Steep turns with and without engine.
16. Climbing turns.
17. Forced landings.
18. Landing with and without engine.
19. Instrument flying under hood.
20. Stopping and starting engine in the air.
21. Taking off and landing across wind.
22. Aerobatics.
23. Air navigation.
24. Forced landing test.
25. Cross-country test.

However, all this had to be co-ordinated with ground training subjects such as the theory of flight, the workings of aero-engines, a knowledge of airframes, armament and so on. The theory of flight was and still is based on three essential factors. First, one needs thrust brought about by the engine(s) to propel the aeroplane into the air. This has to overcome the second factor, which is the drag automatically produced by a heavier-than-air vehicle, for the airframe resists the forces of thrust. Finally, lift is necessary to get the vehicle airborne. This was produced on the biplanes partly by the force of air pushed over the wings from the propeller, but mainly by designing the wings so that a vacuum was created above them as the craft began to roll along the grass. I knew a lot about the theory of flight since I had read it up, but one gained a few more angles in the lecture room. In straight and level flight, for example, pulling back on the joystick causes the nose to rise and the aeroplane to climb. But if you are flying on your back, pulling back on the stick causes the plane to dive towards the ground, which is elementary enough.

More difficult to comprehend is the fact that if one is performing a turn when the wings are at ninety degrees to the ground, then the elevator has the power normally maintained by the rudder, whereas the rudder becomes in effect the elevator. But most important of all were considerations affecting the stall. A stall occurs when drag overcomes lift and thrust, and the aircraft runs out of flying speed. The nose will drop towards the earth and if rudder is then applied the aeroplane will flick into a spin. Depending on the type of aircraft, a spin may take a few hundred feet or many thousand feet before the pilot can recover. Any aeroplane that spins within a couple of hundred feet of the ground generally means that the pilot is on his way to heaven or hell. An inverted spin is the most dangerous attitude of them all. (I gained my nickname 'Dizzy' by managing to put my Spitfire into an inverted spin in 1940. It was even more difficult to recover than to enter such an extraordinary flight attitude.)

For many years during the First World War, no one knew how to get out of a spin. It took scientists such as Tizard and Lindemann, both practising pilots, to find out how to get out of a spin. Since you are nose-diving when spinning, the automatic reaction is to pull hard back on the joystick. However, this merely tightens up the spin and makes it even more difficult to recover. What one does, as the early pioneers found out for me, is to push the stick hard forward, bang on opposite rudder, and hope. But if one is near the ground, hope might spring eternal, but small hope, I fear. Kicking up the daisies is almost inevitable.

Flight Lieutenant Carr first gave me a familiarization flight, showing me the important landmarks for navigational reasons and allowing me to handle the controls. I was pretty raw, especially with the elevators; the nose would jerk up and down, and at one moment we would be looking into the blue sky yonder, and next at the rocky terrain of Perthshire. He would bellow through his Gosport tube to put the starboard wing down, which entailed moving the stick to the right. The starboard aileron would rise and the port aileron would depress, thereby causing drag over the wings which ensured that the starboard wing dropped. The rudder would merely skid the aeroplane left or right depending on which bar the boot gave pressure. But to make a turn with the skid and bank indicator perfectly centred, which I hadn't got a hope of achieving at that stage, required nice positioning of the ailerons, the elevator and the rudder in smooth co-ordination.

When Carr became terrified with my antics, he would inform me that he'd got control, and I would take my fingers and thumbs away from every control within my reach. On one occasion, he slipped the Tiger Moth on to her back, hauled back on the stick and dived vertically for Scone Airport. He levelled out, side-slipped and made a first-class three-point landing – i.e., the wheels and the tail-skid hit the ground at the same moment. He taxied to the hangar area, switched off the magnetos and climbed out on to the wing. He looked into my cockpit and noted that I was covered with vomit.

'I say,' he said, 'I hope you're not going to be one of those air-sick fellows.'

'Well, I've just been sick now, haven't I?' I stated with some asperity.

'Give the rigger half a crown for cleaning up the mess,' he instructed me sternly as he wandered off to the bar.

I gave the rigger sixpence, which was all I could afford. It wasn't pay-day until Friday and I had already run out of money.

Later, Carr told me to buy a large tin of glucose for air-sickness which helped a lot. But I would be air-sick today in a light aircraft despite having flown thousands of hours on Spitfires and jets – more than a hundred aircraft types in fact.

As time went by I began to discover extra-curricular lessons worth learning. On all accounts it was essential to avoid being given a rating as an 'exceptional' pilot at the end of the course, because the tendency then was to take exceptional *ab initio* pilots and groom them to be flying instructors in their own right. The last thing I wanted was to be selected for Flying Training Command.

That Carr was an exceptional pilot was in no doubt, not even in my innocent eyes. He taught me aerobatics – or, as we called them in those days, acrobatics – but I made sure I was never perfect in loops, slow rolls, flick rolls, although I was always in a hurry to get out of a spin, because an aircraft in a spin is literally out of control and I never enjoyed not having full command over my various aeroplanes.

One day he demonstrated a 'dead-stick' landing and finished us up in a field. One had to watch the direction of smoke from chimneys, even the movement of wheat in the fields, to determine how the wind blew. In a light aeroplane such as the Tiger Moth, it is always preferable to land into wind, or as near as possible into wind. On another occasion he was showing me a simulated forced landing with the engine ticking over and not stopped in the air. As the ground got perilously close I suddenly seized control of the Tiger Moth, opened the throttle and climbed like a dingbat.

'What the hell do you think you're doing?' Carr bawled at me over the Gosport tube. I couldn't reply so I pointed vigorously down. Just below us were some very tall electric pylons carrying high-voltage electricity through the cables.

'Don't you think I saw them?' he snapped. He hadn't and I reckon I saved his life – and mine. He didn't discuss the matter when we landed at Scone, proof positive of the pudding, in my view.

He showed me how to get the engine going if it had failed in the air through dirty petrol or something like that. This was a hilarious experience. At about 5,000 feet he stuffed the Tiger Moth on to its back, turned off the two magnetos, and when the prop ceased circulating pulled back on the stick, sending us down in a vertical dive. Without the roar of the engine, all one could hear was the screech of the wind through the rigging wires. When he had attained terminal velocity the propeller was turning like crazy through the wind forces. He snapped on the magneto switches, and she started again as quick as a witch on a broomstick avoiding a bat on a dark night.

Instrument flying was eerie. You pulled over your head a canopy made of green canvas which shut out all outside light. With no visual orientation, all one could do was to trust the instruments implicitly and hope to God that the instructor was keeping a sharp look-out for other aeroplanes. (This didn't happen to one of my friends, and while he was under the hood his aeroplane hit another in midair. He lost both his legs, but went on to fly Spitfires in the war with tin legs; and furthermore, he flew jet fighters with the Royal Auxiliary Air Force after the war.)

When I had achieved five hours' flying with my instructor, Carr decided that I should fly solo, on my very own. He watched me strap myself in, muttered, 'Good luck,' and wandered back to his hut, lighting his pipe as he did so. Flying instructors always try to appear unconcerned when they send their trainees off on their own, but in fact they tremble like they've got St Vitus's dance until he lands safely. Carr didn't fool me! Five hours' dual was pretty fast to be sent solo; some people take eight or even the top limit, ten hours, dual before they are sent off. Some, of course, are never sent solo; they were kicked out; I suppose twenty-five per cent of my course failed to get into the air on their own.

I wasn't afraid to go solo because I thought I would make it. But it was an odd experience when one turned one's head and noted that Carr was not sitting in the back seat. I also observed when I took off that the trim of the aeroplane was slightly affected since there was not a twelve-stone man sitting behind. But as I climbed I felt free as air for the first time – with the blue above and the green below. There was no Gosport tube and there was no Carr bawling down it. If I felt like diving into the ground or colliding with a big Scottish mountain, no one could say nay to me. I climbed to about 5,000 feet, stuffed the nose down and performed a rather nasty loop. This was strictly unauthorized, but no one could see me for there was a layer of thin cloud keeping me invisible from Carr's searching eyes. Then I practised a few side-slips, high above the ground. I loved side-slipping; I even side-slipped the big jet fighters I went on to fly years later. But in the Tiger Moth with its open cockpit, one could feel the gust of air on one's face as one proceeded along sideways, a most exhilarating sensation.

The purpose of side-slipping was to lose height much more quickly than normal; the Tiger Moth, of course, was not possessed of flaps or dive brakes which have a similar effect. The trick was to aim at the point of landing, and if you considered you were too high to touch down at the desired point, then the following action was taken. Push the joystick hard over to port or starboard as required, and then apply full opposite rudder. One could reverse this trend if there were sufficient height before touchdown point. It was a glorious experience.

When I had been in the air for my allotted time, I decided to come in too high on my approach for landing, just to give Carr a fright. At about 500 feet I side-slipped to the right and then to the left, straightened her out and touched down on the grass just alongside Carr's office. It wasn't a bad landing. I taxied her in and Carr came leaping along like an injured rhino.

'What the bloody hell do you think you're doing?' he shrieked.

'Sorry, sir,' I replied. 'I made an error of judgment and had to slip off a bit of height.'

'Slip off a bit!' he screamed. 'You slipped off five hundred feet of bloody height!'

'Well, I got down in one piece, didn't I?' I remarked mildly.

He grunted.

'Come along to the mess,' he said. 'You didn't do my ulcer much good.'

In about 1941 a disillusioned flying instructor, who was also no mean poet, wrote a poem for *Punch*.

An extract reads:

> 'What did you do in the War, Daddy,
> How did you help us to win?'
> 'Circuits and bumps by the score, Laddy,
> And how to get out of a spin.'

Carr did not give me an exceptional assessment, neither did I deserve one. I just wanted to be a fighter pilot.

The course dispersed after two months and we all headed in different directions; a quarter of the pupils who failed the course were sent home and would find themselves liable for conscription in due course. I took a train home on leave and waited for instructions posting me to an Advanced Flying Training School. I didn't have long to wait for documents arrived in short time sending me to RAF Hullavington in Gloucestershire. That wasn't too far away so I packed my bags and drove in my Morgan three-wheel sports car in a westerly direction. The Morgan had two powerful JAP motor-cycle engines in vee format and it was fast although it needed watching since it was unstable.

Hullavington was a regular RAF station, and everyone wandered around in their best uniforms saluting like mad. No one saluted me because although I was now commissioned in the rank of Acting Pilot Officer under Probation, I hadn't got a uniform and wore plain clothes and a flat cap. It was a flying training station but my course was there for square-bashing, learning military law, mess etiquette and so on. I was given a list of rules and regulations and instructed to turn up at the Ground Training School at eight o'clock the next morning. There were some sixty other embryo officers assembled in the room, and I noted that some thieves and rogues had slipped through the mesh; but there were also a few friends of mine from Scone, which pleased me.

In attendance on the aged squadron leader who gave us an introductory address was a gang of travelling tailors from some of the West End shops. The squadron leader explained that we would be given a uniform allowance of about £80, but that in fact would not be enough so we would have to pay for the rest. A travelling tailor from Gieves took hold of me and measured me up and down. I had to obtain two No. 1 uniforms, mess kit, shirts, shoes and other accoutrements according to the standard laid down. (All I felt I needed was a flying suit, and before long I would prove that to be true.) The uniforms would be delivered in a week, the tailor said, and when he and his competitors had finished measuring up the course, they rushed off to London with overladen order books.

Then the squadron leader explained mess etiquette; we weren't to mention a woman's name in the mess; we weren't to discuss politics; we weren't to talk about religion. It seemed to me that I had joined a society of Carthusian monks, which I had in fact in a manner of speaking, as I was to discover in due course. I even had to submit an application to park my car within the station precincts, and if I committed a disciplinary offence, that privilege would be forfeit and I'd have to pay a garage to have it parked. We were now subject to disciplinary procedures and the maximum punishment which could be meted out by the station commander was twenty-eight days confined to camp, meaning one couldn't leave the station. If it came to a court martial, however, having hit a senior officer in the eye or something like that, we could be dismissed the Service or cashiered; in theory the latter meant that the offender would never again be allowed to hold the King's commission in any of the three armed services.

The routine was that we had to attend the parade ground at six-thirty in the morning for physical jerks which would last for approximately an hour. Then we could go to the mess and get cleaned up and ready for breakfast at eight o'clock. The rest of the morning would be spent on the parade ground under the eagle eye of the Station Warrant Officer and his drill sergeants. Lunch would be at one o'clock and afterwards we would be given ground lessons – not on aeroplanes but military procedure – until five o'clock. Assuming it wasn't one's turn to act as Orderly Officer, or Orderly Dog as the chore was termed, we could write a letter home. We were not to leave the station in any case for the first fortnight. If I was Orderly Dog, I would have to inspect the fire picket, see that the prisoners in the cells weren't being beaten up, visit the airmen's mess and ask if everyone was satisfied with the food – they always were, they had to be, even if it was putrid.

It was tough but they relaxed things as time went by, when we used to form gangs and share the cost of taxis to go to places like Cirencester and visit the pubs. I neither drank alcohol nor smoked in those days, so I could sip a lemonade; but I would have to pay for the beer when my turn came around. There were a number of members of the old Commonwealth on the course who had come over to Britain, working their way as ships' stewards or even stokers, to pay for the journey. They were a pretty tough bunch – one-time sheep farmers or even lumberjacks – but all were inspired by the thought of becoming a pilot, apart from the thieves and rogues who had gone into hiding to avoid their creditors.

Our uniforms arrived in due course and we looked rather silly wearing the rank of pilot officer but with no pilots' wings sewn on. But this meant that the airmen round the camp had to salute us. One day I saluted the Station Warrant Officer, who glared at me, stuck his stick under his armpit and bawled while standing strictly to attention:

'Mr Allen, SIR. You don't bloody well salute Warrant Officers! *They salute you!*'

It wasn't quite my scene but I was given an essential grounding. Towards the end of the course our posting orders came through. I was to report to the Advanced Flying Training School at Lossiemouth in Inverness. (Someone must have thought I was a Scotsman, which I'm not . . .) I eagerly inquired what type of training aircraft were on the inventory, and was told that they had North American Harvards, single-engine two-seater monoplanes; and Oxfords, twin-engine monoplanes. I hoped to God that I would be put on to Harvards for that would point me in the direction of Fighter Command, whereas the Oxford would doom me in terms of becoming a bomber, even a seaplane pilot.

I drove home, went to London with my bags, and took a night express to Darkest Scotland.

The Harvard was a low wing monoplane which could achieve about 250 mph on the dive. It was perfectly stable but aerobated well. It had one machine-gun in the wing for gunnery training – if any. Its only disadvantage was that it was the noisiest aircraft in the world on take-off and landing. This was so because it had a tiny steel two-bladed propeller which revved, or the ends of the blades did, at supersonic speed. The pitch of the propeller could be controlled throughout the spectrum, fine pitch, which made the noise, being essential for take-off and for landing in case an overshoot was necessary. (The early Spitfires, when I joined my first squadron, had merely fine pitch for take-off and landing, and coarse pitch for cruising. This was a serious operational handicap, but in due course the pitch could be controlled throughout the spectrum.) It had a radial engine, and the cockpit was comfortable. (Every British aircraft I have flown was acutely uncomfortable, every American aircraft the lap of luxury.) It was not a difficult aircraft to fly, although at first sight the masses of instruments made it seem so. (The Spitfire had only about four vital instruments!) There was a radio-telephone system between the instructor and the trainee, a great advance over the old Gosport tube.

I certainly did not enjoy my advanced flying training. For some reason my flight commander took an instant dislike to me – the feeling was mutual. My flying instructor was a sergeant pilot, and compared with Flight Lieutenant Carr's expertise he was a mere amateur. They gave me a very rough time, but towards the end of the course, the station commander got downwind of a clash of personalities and transferred me to Flight Lieutenant Jamie Rankin's flight. Jamie personally acted as my flying instructor, and he was superb. He went on to become one of the finest fighter pilots of the war. He gave me an Above the Average assessment as a trainee pilot, and strongly recommended that I be posted to a fighter squadron.

The only amusing occurrence during my advanced training was when the visiting Chief Flying Instructor from the Central Flying School gave me my passing-out test. When we landed he said:

'You fly all right. But you don't turn your head frequently enough to see behind. When you get engaged with the Luftwaffe, you'll get bullets up your bum if you don't take care. Mark my words.'

At the height of the Battle of Britain he was commanding a squadron in 11 Group, which my squadron relieved. I discovered that he had been shot down on three or four occasions, clearly not having seen what hit him. I approached him.

'Remember me, sir?' I inquired.

'Vaguely,' he replied.

'Well, you gave me a flying test and warned me that I would get bullets up my bum. How many bullets have you had up your bum lately?'

2

No. 66 (Fighter) Squadron

There is a proverb which tell us that fortune favours the brave. But I don't consider that I ever was particularly brave, so more apt, perhaps, is another proverb which says fortune favours fools. I left Lossiemouth and went home on leave and waited, while the April showers of 1940 brought along the spring flowers. My mother was juddering slightly because she knew what I was waiting for, and it arrived in the hands of a telegraph boy, whom I intercepted before she saw him.

The telegram was succinct and to the point: 'Report to the No. 66 Fighter Squadron based at RAF Duxford pm on 13 April'. I think 13 April was a Friday, but I was not superstitious at that time, although I used to positively clutch at straws within weeks of receiving the telegram, which changed my whole lifestyle.

I didn't know where Duxford was, but when I looked at the maps, I found it just to the south of Cambridge. Nor did I know what type of aircraft No. 66 Squadron had on its inventory – they could have been Hurricanes, which simply did not appeal to me in any way. On the other hand, they might be Spitfires, which appealed to me very much. I had seen the Spitfire in flight, I had seen photographs of it, to me it was the very pink of perfection – and after due experience, it proved to me that it was indeed perfection. My Spitfires, and I flew the whole range more or less, starting with the Mk I and finishing with the Mk 23, let me down on only two occasions in some 6,000 take-offs and landings. Once when a pilot had previously made a heavy landing but was either too scared, or daft, to report it to the aircraft fitters, which meant that one of my undercarriage oleo legs would not come down on selection. I had no option except to land it on one wheel, and the airframe toppled towards the end of the landing run – but it did hardly any damage to the aircraft. And on another occasion, I burst a tyre on landing – and it was a good landing, so I think the tyre should take the blame for that, rather than the Spitfire. (It was impossible to diagnose why tyres burst on landing, because they are carefully inspected after every landing an aircraft makes.) But my Spitfire Mk 9B finished up a bit of a wreck after the tyre burst. Of course, I wrote off a number of Spitfires in due course, about a dozen I guess, but they were written off through battle damage, which could hardly be the fault of Supermarines,* or their brilliant senior designer, R. J. Mitchell. He died as a comparatively young man, but he lived long enough to see his prototype Spitfire take to the air, and like Phoebus it arose and painted the sable skies with azure, white and red.

I had 64 hours 19 minutes dual, and 145 hours 16 minutes solo marked in my pilot's flying log-book when I packed my uniforms in my suitcases and set course for Duxford. My kit would hardly fit into my Morgan. As I arrived at the hangars at Duxford, I could see nothing but Spitfires littering the airfield – not a Hurricane in sight. Wherever Heaven is, St Peter opened the doors when I arrived at Duxford. Yet curiously, the Devil was also rubbing his hands with glee, for he dropped me into Hell using the same site – Duxford.

The Morgan began losing oil on the drive, and I stopped and filled the sump twice. She still smelled hot, and sure enough came to a grinding halt just by the sergeants' mess. I managed to swing her into the car-park while she still had some momentum, and perforce had to carry my bags to the officers' mess, some 200 yards away. What a manner in which to arrive at one's first fighter station! A mess steward gave me a hand with my bags when I nearly broke the main doors of the mess on entry, and escorted me to the Mess

* Supermarine Company, a subsidiary of Vickers, who manufactured the Spitfire.

Secretary's office. I told him who I was; he already knew as it so happened, and he allocated me a room and a batman. The mess was still running according to pre-war standards, and it was indeed a most comfortable, quite large hotel, capable of accommodating more than a hundred officers, and with the RAF equivalents of major-domos, butlers, waiters, and personal valets. In the course of the war all that changed, of course, and hard living became the norm.

'I'm afraid you'll have to share a batman,' the Mess Secretary, a retired squadron leader, told me gloomily.

I inwardly burst into laughter.

'That's a bad show,' I replied rather haughtily.

'Isn't it? But there we are. Sorry about that.'

'I expect I'll just be able to cope,' I said.

Fortunately my half-batman appeared at that moment and escorted me to my room, humping my bags simultaneously.

The room was large and comfortable with built-in hanging cupboards, a wash-hand basin with what estate agents like to term a toilet cabinet attached to the wall above. Apart from the fact it had a mirror on the front, it wasn't much use to me since I used a primitive, by today's standards, electric razor. I also had a hand-propelled razor driven by a tiny fly-wheel, which gained its momentum when you squeezed and released a lever. (Later, I made the attempt to use it on the first battle climb of the day, so when that fell sergeant Death, who is indeed quick in his arrest, tried to cut my head off with his scythe, my head would fall into the basket clean-shaven. He made many attempts, but he has missed – so far. I had to give that practice up when I found that my bristles tended to fall into my oxygen mask. My sole and single life-line on countless occasions was pure oxygen.)

My batman showed me the bathrooms, nice and handy from my room, sparklingly clean, and there were cubicles with showers if one preferred. I slipped a visiting card into the holder made for it on my bedroom door indicating to anyone who might be interested that the room was now

occupied by Pilot Officer H. R. Allen, Royal Air Force, and
left my half-batman, Jones, to unpack my bags. He didn't
know, nor did I, that we would be together for a long time. I
glanced at the card on the door of the room opposite mine,
which announced sternly that the occupant was Squadron
Leader R. H. A. Leigh; the footnote at the bottom informed
me that he was a member of the Royal Air Force Club. God
knows what they do today, but it was *de rigueur* in those
faraway ages to let all and sundry know on your card which
club(s) you belonged to. This Leigh, I reasoned, must be my
squadron commander, for that particular wing of the mess
was occupied only by the officers of No. 66 Squadron. I also
appreciated, as an officer of what the Army term 'field rank'
– majors and lieutenant-colonels – that he would be the
tenant of two rooms, not just one like me, for such
dignitaries were allowed a sitting-room-cum-study alongside
their bedrooms – i.e. a suite. I wondered what sort of chap he
was, and that didn't take me long to find out. Today, nearly
forty years on, he is still one of my oldest and closest friends.
'Forty years on, growing older and older,/Shorter in wind, as
in memory long,/Feeble of foot and rheumatic of
shoulder,/What will it help you that once you were strong?'
God knows: I don't.

By now I knew the etiquette in the military genre – my parents
had indicated the way in what might be termed the civilian
chiaroscuro. So as I wandered down the stairs, along the long
corridor to the main hall of the mess, I paused by the discreet
table which supported the visitors' book, the mess members'
book, and signed in as a member of the officers' mess at RAF
Duxford. (Army and RAF messes were modelled on London
clubs; the Navy as usual do things differently, and have places
they prefer to call ward-rooms, reminiscent of wardrobes.
Nor do the Navy have lavatories; you either go to the 'heads'
or piddle over the side of the ship.) On the table were two small
silver salvers, and I by then knew what they were all about – in
any case, discreet notices attached indicated what they were

all about. So I 'dropped my card' in them, one addressed to the Station Commander, and I sincerely hoped he was unmarried for an awful number of RAF wives are akin to domesticated marsupials; the other to the President of the Mess Committee, who was a kind of executive director of a quite large hotel. I had no idea, of course, that as the years rolled on, I would be handed the position as PMC to a dozen or so officers' messes.

But the most important thing on my mind was to see if I could salvage my Morgan tricycle car, so I marched to the sergeants' mess car-park to evaluate the situation. On the way, airmen and NCOs saluted me after a hard day's work, and although I returned their salutes, I had merely driven from Surrey to Duxford. One airman gave me the 'eyes right' because he was carrying his tea-mug and his cutlery in his right hand, silly ass – if he had held them in his left hand, he could have given a conventional salute. On the other hand, he might have sprained his wrist, in which case full marks for initiative.

When I arrived at the Morgan, I found the engine in pieces and a gang of senior NCOs closely examining the wreckage with interest.

'Hey! That's my car,' I said.

'I know that, sir,' the leader of the gang replied. 'I saw you glide into the car-park. I've done a strip inspection. One of your pistons has seized up.'

'But I've only got two pistons,' I remarked.

The gang grinned.

'We could probably patch it up in station workshops,' the senior fitter suggested. 'We'd have to do the job after working hours, of course, not to encroach on Air Force time and all that. But we'd have to put a new sleeve into the cylinder. We'd certainly need to make new rings for the piston.'

'How much?' I inquired.

'No more than a fiver.'

I looked at the Morgan and pondered. It was a good car. But supposing the squadron was redeployed to another station, and I had to fly a Spitfire in squadron formation. How would I get the car to the next station? Anyway, it was too small. I came to a decision.

'Anyone like to buy it?' I asked.

'Yes, sir. I'll buy it,' the senior fitter replied. 'I'll give you forty-five quid for it.'

'Done,' I said. 'It's yours.'

'Trouble is, I can only afford to give you five quid a month.'

'OK. That's a deal.'

Within the next nine months, No. 66 Squadron was deployed and redeployed to nine different RAF stations. Come hell or high water, come bombing and strafing attacks on the various airfields, once every month that RAF sergeant posted me a cheque for five pounds until he had cleared the debt. Furthermore, the various postmen delivered every one of his letters to me.

How's that for integrity?

The next morning, and I was due to report formally to my squadron commander at 8.30 a.m., I had a bath at an early hour and was returning to my room in my dressing gown, carrying a sponge-bag, when I perceived a large, bulky man approaching the bathrooms, swinging his own sponge-bag in his hand. Normal enough, you might think, apart from the fact he was stark bollock naked. I stared at this unusual apparition.

'Good morning,' it said.

I did not reply and walked past it wondering whether I had joined a nudist colony.

An hour or so later I reported to the squadron adjutant's office, to be greeted by an old man wearing the brevet of the Royal Flying Corps, sewn on to a flight lieutenant's uniform.

'Pilot Officer Allen reporting, sir,' I said.

'For God's sake don't call me sir. I'm Pat Hewitt, dug out and brought back for the war. Everything all right so far?'

'So far, yes. But there's a lot to learn.'

He looked me up and down, taking quick note whether my buttons were polished well enough and that I hadn't got mud on my shoes. Then he walked to the inner door, opened it, and

I heard him say that a new pilot had arrived and that the file was there in the 'In' tray. Then he ushered me into a haze of tobacco smoke which made me cough and splutter; at the time I didn't smoke but, as Ovid said, *Tempus edax rerum*. I managed to come to a halt before I barged into the desk and vaguely made out the large form of the nudist I had briefly encountered an hour or so earlier. He was now dressed in the uniform of a squadron leader, and was stretched languidly behind his desk.

'Take a pew,' he said, indicating an uncomfortable chair.

I saluted smartly, removed my hat – or cap, as the military prefer to call their headgear – and perched myself in an erect sitting posture. Rupert – his name – eyed me, and his eyes reminded me of a cod just beginning to suffer rigor mortis after death. It was an expression he could turn on according to his whimsy, and today he has by no means lost the art. What is even more disconcerting is the fact that he has the ability to put on a straight poker face simultaneously, which is why he is such a good poker player.

'Good morning,' he said.

'Good morning, sir,' I replied.

'Thanks. I note that you do not always give a response when someone gives you a good-morning.'

'Sorry, sir.' My mind worked furiously, then it spewed out a suggested solution.

'The trouble is,' I replied, 'I never talk to anyone before breakfast. This was instilled into me by my father. It's a bit rude, perhaps, but I can't help it.'

His eyes lit up; they were blue and seemed to protrude slightly from their sockets.

'Funny thing that, old boy,' he said. 'I never talk to anyone before breakfast either. It really gives me a pain to even have to say good-morning to people before breakfast. But you know, *toujours la politesse* and all that.'

'My family motto, sir, I fear,' I replied, 'is bugger *la politesse*.'

His eyes became cod-like for a moment, then quick as the

whores' drawers come down on boat-race night, his face lined
with a grin, he opened his mouth, threw back his head, opened
his mouth wider, thereby displaying his tobacco-stained,
widely dispersed teeth, and laughed like a stallion neighing.
Then he composed himself, put on a straight face reminiscent
of an Egyptian mummy, and got down to business.

He's a great guy is Rupert. He was my mentor and, before
very many months were out, we would become comrades in
arms *par excellence*.

In those days, battledress had not been thought of, so we
always wore No. 1 Dress, or best-blue, even when flying,
except for those occasions when we flew in shirt-sleeves, flying
overalls, or even pyjamas. One No. 1 uniform was kept in
good shape for ceremonies such as funerals when one of us
would be detailed to attend the burial of his best friend; we
never held formal parades in the war. The single difference
between formal dress and working uniform was that, for the
latter, we wore forage caps and not 'hats' glittering with gold
braid surrounding the RAF albatross. Forage caps were
excellent headgear which could be stuffed into one of the
capacious pockets of your tunic; in theory, when they were
unbuttoned, they could be pulled over the head to keep the
ears warm. We used to call them an unrepeatable name which
rhymes with 'hunt-caps', and there was a good enough reason
for using that expression which I cannot, in all decency,
explain. I was shocked when it was decided to do away with
forage caps some time after the war ended. They were smart
enough and practical but, even more, they were about the only
item of uniform which the RAF retained from the days of the
Royal Flying Corps, which was father to the RAF – its mother
was the Royal Naval Air Service. But then, constant changes
have been made in RAF uniform, very few of which were for
the better.

After my formal interview with my squadron commander,
I returned to the mess to change out of my best uniform,
adjusted my forage cap and visited the flying clothes stores.

There I was issued with the bulky, rubber-lined Irving flying overalls – which I hardly ever wore; a leather Irving jacket with heavy wool lining, most useful for wandering around the squadron dispersal in cold weather, but not the slightest use when flying the Spitfire, for the cockpit was too narrow and the jacket too bulky to squeeze oneself in; but the Hurricane boys could climb into their more capacious cockpits wearing them, and the leather was so thick that it was quite useful as armour-plate against small pieces of flying lead in combat. Leather gauntlets were essential, so were the silk inner gloves to insulate the hands against temperatures of minus fifty degrees at 30,000 feet and above. Thick woollen stockings, together with suede flying boots, wool-lined, were equally essential.

Then I had to go to the specialist equipment sections. I was fitted with a leather flying helmet, an oxygen mask which was fixed on one side, but with push-button clips on the other so one could bawl at the ground crew until the engine was running, then clip the mask on and tighten the straps to ensure that there were no outside air leaks. Radio earphones were tested and inserted into the earpieces of the helmet, and the wiring system was connected to the microphone in the oxygen mask. The Germans used throat microphones which transmitted from the vocal cords, not the tongue, in certain respects a more effective method than ours. Then there followed a visit to the parachute store to be fitted so the straps were adjusted exactly: not too tight to make for discomfort; not so slack that one would move off the shoulder and send you hurtling to your doom on bailing out. The parachute store was a tall building where fully extended parachutes could be hung from the ceiling to dry out. There were double doors to the store to ensure that the temperature and humidity in the building were maintained exactly according to the strict requirements. Every month your parachute had to be returned to the store for drying out, close examination and repacking. It was rather amusing, necessary as the inspections were, for what happened to our parachutes, placed in the Spitfires with cockpit canopies open to the rain and the elements in general, was nobody's business.

Sensible people kept their parachutes in our tall, steel, flying-clothing lockers – assuming we had lockers, and on many occasions we did not have lockers. Before the break of dawn, and depending on the weather, I would carry my parachute out to my Spitfire, and place it on the wing-tip with the straps carefully arranged to hang down for ease of buckling them onto one's body. Some pilots preferred to place them on the pilot's seat in the cockpit, but I reckoned that since it was necessary to strap on my safety harness in the cockpit after buckling on the parachute, confusion might arise *vis-à-vis* one set of straps and the other. In those days, our parachutes were manufactured by the Irving Company and made of pure silk. Later in the war, I believe that man-made fibres were used. There was an awful lot of silk to a parachute, and in the course of duty I once had occasion to steal my half-wrecked parachute; from the remnants, I managed to have made three pyjama suits, very smooth to the body, highly sophisticated.

If you had to bail out in action to save your life, and details had to be authenticated, the Irving Company made you a member of the Caterpillar Club. When I was officially accepted as a member of the club, they sent me a small model of a caterpillar made of pure gold. On the back was inscribed 'P.O. H. R. Allen, October 1940'. If you bailed out when your aircraft was on fire, the golden caterpillar's eyes were made of red semi-precious stone. If not on fire, they were coloured green. Mine had green eyes, although I believe my Spitfire was on fire but I couldn't remember; I was in a hurry to get out. I gave the little brooch to my wife in due course, and she used to wear it on appropriate occasions. It is now lost beyond redemption. Heavens knows how or where.

Caterpillar is the popular name for the larvae of butterflies, moths, and saw-flies. Rather appropriate for an aviator to be associated with the genus, especially as I received my *ab initio* flying training on the Tiger Moth.

Curiouser and curiouser!

3

B Flight

Rupert disposed of me to B Flight; there were only two flights on the squadron, A and B. I asked the Stores NCO to assemble all my flying kit and have it sent in a van to B Flight, then I telephoned and asked for squadron transport to drive me to B Flight, which was alongside A Flight, on the other side of the airfield, a good mile away from the hangar area and the administrative buildings. Duxford had no runways at that time; the Spitfires operated from grass, taking the full length of the airfield if the wind was slack according to the wind-sock. One could diagnose the strength of the wind in the terms that if the wind-sock was hanging limply, there was no wind worth consideration; but if the sock was stretched to its uttermost limits, the wind might be up to gale force, when it was essential to take off and land straight into wind. Halfway house lay somewhere between these extremes as indicated by the wind-sock. Around the perimeter of the airfield was a narrow concrete road, sufficiently wide for large petrol bowsers to make their way to the squadron from the underground petrol tanks, which were sited discreetly to avoid damage in case the whole lot blew up for some reason.

There was nothing like an air traffic control tower at Duxford, and take-offs and landings were made by guess and by God, with the nominal assistance of a duty pilot, whose only aids consisted of an Aldis lamp which could flash green for OK, red for danger, or white for some unknown reason. He sat in a wooden shed with a telephone, a Very pistol and little else. We all had to take turns at being 'air traffic controllers', also officers in charge of night flying. If the wind came from the appropriate direction, and was strong enough to warrant it, we had to make a very short take-off pointing directly at the hangars. Many's the time I nearly removed the hangar roof, or even the whole range of hangars, especially when taking off before dawn. The messes, barrack blocks, cookhouses and so forth were sited away from the airfield across a quite busy main road leading from Royston to Cambridge. Consequently, everyone had to walk across the road to get to their domestic quarters. I thought of setting up a couple of machine-gun posts to fire warning shots over the heads of half-witted motorists who maintained their speed at over 60 mph as they approached the obviously busy camp. But no one took my suggestion seriously – they lacked my imagination, I fear.

B Flight consisted of two long wooden sheds, one for the pilots, the other where the NCOs had their tiny offices, the remainder being used by the airmen. The flight commander's 'office' comprised a bell-tent, and as I opened the flap and entered, there was a small desk and a couple of wicker easy chairs. Behind the desk was seated Flight Lieutenant Billy Burton. The form was that you saluted your flight commander and called him 'sir', first thing in the morning and last thing when the working day ended – sometimes the working day did not end until dawn broke on the following day. So I naturally saluted him and told him that PO Allen had been detailed to join his flight. He gazed at me calmly without even shuddering at the prospect. Open on his desk was my flying log-book which had been sent over by the squadron adjutant. He made no comment as to my above-the-average assessment as a pilot; he was obviously going to confirm that for himself. He stood to shake hands and beckoned me to sit down. He was quite short, tough, erect, a gentleman, a product of a public school and the RAF Officers' Cadet School at Cranwell. I suppose he was aged twenty-five, beating me in years by five and in flying experience by a factor of five or more.

Billy by no means shot a barrage of questions at me. He mildly asked me some questions as to the theory of flight, especially in monoplanes. (It wasn't all that long ago that No. 66 Squadron had re-equipped from biplane Gauntlets to

Spitfires. It was the second Spitfire squadron in history. The pioneers were serving with the opposition, No. 19 Squadron, also based at Duxford.) Did I know all about incipient spins?

'Yes,' I replied. 'If I'm daft enough to stall on the approach and push on too much rudder at the same time, then I would find myself in an incipient spin. Added to which, I would be a dead duck.'

He nodded in grave acquiescence.

'That about sums it up,' he said.

He made no attempt to interrogate me as to my social background and suchlike topics, but he was clearly summing up a newly joined young man and trying to decide whether I would be good enough or useless. At the same time, I was also summing him up for what he was worth, and in the end he was worth quite a lot, although he had a shaky time before he was killed in action, performing most gallantly. But he obviously wanted to confirm that I knew what I was doing, because there were no dual-controlled Spitfires, and my first flight would be as solo as it ever was on the Tiger Moth, more so in fact, because my instructor had made quite sure I could fly the dual-controlled Moth on my own before he sent me solo.

Whatever doubts he might have had, he informed me that I was detailed to fly one of his Spitfires that afternoon, and that he would give me a conducted tour of the cockpit before take-off. He took a map of the area from a drawer in his desk, laid it out and showed me the important navigational features in the region. Most obvious was the town of Cambridge, since the airfield was about five miles to the south of the city. (Matthew Arnold wrote of 'that sweet city with her dreaming spires', referring to Oxford before Lord Nuffield established a motor-car industry on the outskirts. Pity he made no reference to King's College, Cambridge, which whacks any Oxford College hollow.) The low-lying fen country to the north was featureless, apart from one magnificent visual homing aid. This was the Bedford River which runs in an absolutely straight line from Downham Market to Earith. If one was hopelessly lost, as I often was, it wasn't very difficult to find

the Wash and pinpoint King's Lynn. From there, the Great
Ouse led one to the unmistakable Bedford River, which must
surely be in truth a canal – no river I know flows in such a
straight line for so many miles – and then one could get re-
orientated. Railway lines were of very little value in East
Anglia for navigational purposes, but in other parts of the
country they most certainly were, provided you had the
ability to fly low enough to read the names of the stations!
Billy also informed me of the hazards of the peculiar weather
in the East Anglian area. Thunderstorms tend to hang around
for hours there, head away somewhere or other, and then
return. The marshy fenland brought with it surface fog in
dawn and dusk conditions when the skies were clear, and thin
fog could cover the airfield very quickly indeed. The fog might
rise to only ten feet, but ten feet was critical for landing, and it
is most difficult to keep an aircraft straight after touchdown
when visibility is a mere ten yards.

I had always been interested in meteorology, I used to read
books on the subject when a boy. I would watch the slow
changing of cloud formations which, when speeded up on film
showing the changes which occur in twelve hours in half a
minute on the screen, is dramatic. We were taught the basics
of Met forecasting at our flying training schools, but the
lectures were not particularly helpful to me, because I knew
more about these things than my instructors, partly by
instinct. A good sea captain learns the rudiments of his craft
best by sailing as a boy, and finding out how to tie knots as a
midshipman at the age of thirteen. A good soldier must know
about the landscape, about features on the ground which
make for the best offensive, or defensive, positions. A good
airman must lie on his back on the ground and observe the air,
the birds, and most especially the clouds. I spent a lot of time
simply gazing into the air when I was a boy. I knew that the
original Met forecaster was Jean Baptiste, a French biologist,
who systematically classified cloud formations in 1801-4.
There are three basic clouds which he named: cirrus – very
high; cumulus – big or small bubbly clouds; and stratus – low,

menacing, deadly clouds. He proposed four additional compound formations, cirro-cumulus; cirro-stratus; cumulo-stratus; and cumulo-cirro-stratus or nimbus – great thunderclouds which can stretch up to 40,000 feet in our climes, or 60,000 feet during the monsoon season in eastern parts; and they can break an aircraft into tiny pieces if the pilot is fool enough to enter them, through the sheer power of their vicious turbulence.

I learned my craft the hard way. At one time I must have been the finest Met forecaster in Europe, and I proved it on innumerable occasions. During my career as a fighter pilot, the weather was my worst enemy. To be effective, you must first conquer your enemy.

Billy took me along to the pilots' hut to introduce me and give me my bearings. There were only a dozen or so pilots in the shack, which contained beds, a dartboard, a tea urn, trestle tables, a cabinet for maps, and a dozen large, steel flying-clothing lockers. The walls of the room were covered with charts showing silhouettes of aircraft, both German and British – the British Hampden bomber bore a certain resemblance to the German Flying Pencil, the Dornier 17, and it would not be a good thing to shoot down a Hampden believing it to be a Do-17. Magazines were scattered around on the tables, and some pilots were giving them a cursory glance, while others were playing darts or snoozing on their beds. Our main job at that time was patrolling coastal convoys, but a pair of pilots were at fifteen-minutes' readiness, ready to be brought up to immediate readiness on an interception sortie if the scramble order became imminent.

Nearly half the pilots were of senior NCO rank, the rest were officers. Billy introduced me, and they gazed at me languidly. Just another bog-rat, they thought, but we'll have to see how he shapes up. Newly joined pilot officers were considered to be the scum of the earth before the war, and old habits died hard even though the war had by then been proceeding for eight months. Before the war, no one even talked to a bog-rat until he had been on the squadron for six months; they just ignored him. It was quite a good tradition, but it couldn't possibly last when the heat of war struck. Pilot Officer Cooke was brisk, enthusiastic, an experienced pilot by the standards of the day, had thin hair tending to baldness, and a charming smile. He would before long achieve the rank of flight lieutenant, would be awarded the DFC, and would suffer burns in September 1940.

Peter Studd was to become my best friend on the squadron, and I was destined to attend his funeral in August. He was a tall, gangly young man, quite rich, a bit of a *poseur*, a good fighter pilot, and he had a flash sports car. He was a gourmet, and we used to drive to various hotels for a meal, when we could get away from the camp, and we enjoyed each other's company. He was shot down by a gunner in a German bomber, and floated ashore a week later, green, bloated and decaying. He was too enthusiastic – never get too close to enemy bombers unless on a beam or high-quarter attack.

Johnnie Mather was there, a pilot officer, fair hair, tall, slim, with a great sense of humour. He was destined to suffer anoxia – lack of oxygen – at 30,000 feet in September. Most probably his oxygen tube became disconnected as he turned his head so violently to scan for the enemy at the rear. I saw his Spitfire begin to bank over, I chased it down as it went into a nose-dive. I shouted at him over the R/T in an attempt to help him regain consciousness. I was dead unlucky, and Johnnie was dead, making a grave thirty feet under the sod for his Spitfire and for himself.

A. N. R. L. Appleton was there, a pilot officer, a smiling, curly-headed young man with much charm. What happened to Apple I just don't remember, but he was a good guy to have around. Sergeant Pilot Duggie Hunt was there, a pretty experienced fighter pilot, salt of the earth, crinkled hair, bushy eyebrows. He didn't know, nor did I, that I would get command of the squadron before a year was out, that I would arrange for him to be made a warrant officer, or that I would make the fruitless attempt to get him appointed as my flight commander. Anyway, Duggie did OK. He retired from the RAF in the rank of wing commander; justice is sometimes achieved.

Billy Burton asked Hugh Kennard to take me under his wing and make the attempt to turn me into a fighter pilot. Hugh was a senior pilot officer, and exceptional pilot, a deb's delight, fair-haired, good looking, with an aquiline nose, a great sense of humour, and in the course of time became a shrewd businessman. He left No. 66 Squadron shortly before the heat really came on, and I often wonder how he would have shaped up if he had been allowed to stay with us. I think that he would have got himself killed in very short time, or he would have become an accredited ace – don't ask me why I hold those views because I don't know. They were just my prophecies.

Having allocated me a flying-clothing locker to store my parachute and other accoutrements in, Billy then took me along to meet some of the NCOs who were the backbone of the squadron. These men had all been trained in their craft at the RAF Technical School, Halton, near Wendover. This was the best aeronautical polytechnic in the world at that time. Such men were highly skilled fitters, any one of them could have run a garage standing on his head – and gained a great deal more money than the RAF ever gave them in the process. To gain entry to Halton, you had to be possessed of so many, what we call today, O-levels. Then it was necessary to persuade strict selection boards that you were of the requisite very high calibre. Then the apprentices' were put through a course on the theory and practice of aeroplane engineering which made so many demands that most youngsters today would find the task impossible, not to exclude drill or 'square-bashing', nor the principles of Air Force law and so on. I cannot remember one such man letting me down, during the period when I commanded five fighter squadrons. They were totally reliable, ingenious, good disciplinarians, prepared to die under bombing raids to ensure the serviceability of their aircraft; in short, they were magnificent. I met Corporal Kelly when I joined No. 66 Squadron. Little did he know that within a year he would be made my senior flight-sergeant in charge of aircraft servicing, with twenty-four Spitfires under his technical control. Nor did I.

That afternoon, Billy accompanied me to a Spitfire. Each aircraft had the manufacturer's number on its tail-fin, but the large code letters for No. 66 Squadron, painted on the fuselage, were LZ. This particular Spitfire bore the code letters LZ-X. The fuselage and wing surfaces were camouflaged to meld with fields on the upper surfaces but the wings underneath were painted black on one wing and white on the other. (The camouflage was nothing like as good as that on the Messerschmitt 109, as I was to discover to my cost.) I strapped on my parachute, climbed onto the port wing, and hauled myself into the narrow cockpit. There was a small hatch to assist the process of embarking, which had to be bolted in position when the engine was started.

The first thing that struck me about the Spitfire was the unusual smell as one plonked oneself down on the seat. It was a mixture of 100-octane petrol from the priming pump, hand controlled for starting; and of engine oil; and of dope which was applied to the canvas which concealed the gun-ports – the canvas, of course, vanished into thin air when the eight Browning machine-guns were fired, and when landing after action there was a veritable howl as the aircraft stalled onto the ground in a landing configuration and the air swooped through the now open gun-ports.

Billy told me all about the layout in the cockpit, how to start the engine, what the Spitfire's flying characteristics were, what her maximum speed was on the dive, and so on. As I remember, she would pull off the ground at 70 mph, her approach speed was about 90 mph, and she would be ready for touchdown at 70 mph. Billy did not realize that on the dive the Spitfire could almost reach the speed of sound before her wings fell off. Few people, the boffins apart, had heard of Ernst Mach, an Austrian professor of mathematics, who later specialized in philosophy. He first proposed the theory, now commonplace, that the ratio of speed of a flying body to that of sound should be discussed as its Mach number. The speed of sound varies, depending mostly on the temperature of the air – at height, the air is considerably colder than near to the Earth's surface. The mean speed of sound is 1,120 feet per second. I didn't know anything about Dr Mach either, but I certainly exceeded the speed of sound in my jet fighters, never on propeller-driven aircraft.

When Billy had leapt off the wing of LZ-X, I studied the cockpit layout more carefully and attempted to memorize what he had told me. The first obvious feature was a large black lever to the right, and one had to pump this back and forward about thirty times to get the undercarriage retracted. Above were the oil pressure and fuel availability gauges, also the engine boost gauge, the radiator temperature gauge, and the engine rev counter. In the middle of the instrument panel were the turn and slip indicator, the rate of climb and descent indicator, the artificial horizon, the gyro-compass, the all-essential air speed indicator, the altimeter – which had to be adjusted on the ground depending on the prevailing air pressure as pronounced by the Met people. Above by the wind-shield was the gun-sight, below was the compass proper, and to the left stupid things such as the flying position indicator; and the important flap control. It was all a hazy blur to me when I entered the cockpit for the first time, but in retrospect it was a fairly simple layout.

I gave the ground crew the thumbs-up signal when I had sorted myself out, they retreated while I started the Merlin, I watched the instruments indicating that the engine was warming up satisfactorily, they heaved the enormous starter battery a safe distance away, and I then waved my hands over my face indicating that the chocks should be pulled away from the tyres. I had made sure that the brakes were locked on, also that the pneumatic gauge was indicating a satisfactory reading of compressed air – the brakes, the guns and the undercarriage system depended entirely on compressed air contained in a quite small metal bottle, kept under constant pressure while the engine was running. (In due course I came to the conclusion that having all these essential features controlled by a small compressed-air cylinder made for a fault in design. I was more than convinced when a member of the Luftwaffe shot me up, and I had no guns, no flaps, no undercarriage – sans teeth, sans eyes, sans taste, sans everything. He bust my air bottle.)

The handle of the engine throttle on the Spitfire Mk I was made of bone. When wearing gauntlets that didn't mean very much; but when bare-handed, the feeling of bone became most important, smooth, shiny; and it warmed, the longer the hand controlled the lever. The Spitfire Mk II was given a throttle handle made of wood, but to me the difference was of great dimensions; it somehow seemed to be that mass production had overtaken individual craftsmanship, which of course it had. Silly little thing maybe, but I felt most strongly about it.

As I manipulated that throttle handle to get LZ-X moving towards the point of take-off, the great surge of power from the Rolls-Royce engine impressed me immediately. Having arrived at the point of take-off, as per the wind-sock, I warily opened the throttle further and further until the Merlin engine showed full boost on the supercharger gauge. The engine developed 1,030 horse-power, and as each 'horse' began to pull, the torque on the rudder bars increased greatly. Gingerly, I eased the joy-stick back, and she grumbled as she left terra firma. I gained a little height, attempted to keep the nose in a climbing posture, selected undercarriage up, and pumped like mad on the big black lever to retract the undercart. She nosed up and down as I did this, being extremely sensitive fore and aft – dangerously so, in fact; a few weeks later, modifications had to be made to place weights within the elevator controls, to cut down on her sensitivity in the lateral plane. Eventually, I felt a bang as the undercarriage receded into its cells, and the covers automatically clamped over the wheels. The green lights were out, the red lights were on, meaning that the undercart was firmly up and locked. From that moment on, the Spitfire transformed itself from a pinioned duck into a wild goose.

I climbed her to 20,000 feet; it took 13 minutes, whereas the Hurricane needed 17 minutes, a vital tactical difference indeed, which the Air Staff failed to appreciate. I put my oxygen onto emergency flow, and the gas cooled my tongue and made my throat feel dry, but I realized that my life-line was intact, so I turned the flow back to conserve oxygen. The panorama of the green fen landscape expanded in my vision as I gained height; fortunately visibility was good. I could make out Cambridge, Ely with its great cathedral, Peterborough, as I gained height to the north. Then the bulge of the East Anglian coast came into view and I headed for the distinctive Wash and saw King's Lynn. A coastal convoy was apparently stationary near Great Yarmouth, but I knew Duxford-based Spitfires would be patrolling it. Then I flew out to sea; I had plenty of height if my engine failed and I had to glide back to base. The Merlin was purring away and I daringly switched off one of the magnetos, whereupon the instrument panel shuddered as one bank of cylinders stopped functioning. I turned on that bank, and cut out the other; the rev counter showed a decrease of 300 engine revs, nicely within the limits, and I turned on the switch again. Then I experimented in trimming the rudder and elevator bias and attempted to let the aircraft fly with my hands off the control column. I had to make further minute adjustments before she would fly straight and level, hands off.

I opened the throttle, flung on hard right aileron, maintained the pressure until she was on her back, then I centralized the controls. She didn't like it, and the engine began to splutter because negative gee was not allowing the petrol to feed the carburettors. I pulled the stick back which

gave positive gee and the engine functioned correctly again
as she dropped into a loop off the top of the roll. She
gathered speed very quickly, and I watched with awe the air
speed indicator indicating greater and greater speed. At
something over 450 mph, I hauled back on the stick and she
zoomed up into a loop. I rolled her on the vertical climb and
she responded, light as a feather. As we continued to climb
vertically, I watched the ASI, caught her just before the stall
and kicked the port rudder bar. She put a wing down and I
dived her again as she stall-turned at the end of the zoom
climb. I tried her out on some rolls as she gathered speed
vertically downwards. This was my new toy, and a most
excellent toy it was.

In due course, I returned to base, joined circuit anti-
clockwise, put the undercarriage down when I was
downwind on the circuit, turned in for the final approach
and lowered the flaps. She touched down on three points,
bumped into the air again slightly, and then plonked her tail
wheel firmly onto the grass. The long nose of the Spitfire
reared up, and I had to stick my head out of the by now open
canopy to maintain a straight landing course. I eventually
squeezed on the brakes when I reckoned that she wouldn't
topple onto her nose because of over-use of the brakes. She
came to a halt, whereupon I gave her a burst of throttle and
steered her using the brakes to the perimeter track. I taxied
back to B Flight dispersal, very carefully swinging her nose
to port and starboard so as to see obliquely ahead, watching
out for obstructions. Then I parked her within the line of
Spitfires on the grass near the flight huts and shut off the
engine.

The Spitfire was perfection. She dived like a cormorant.
And I had mastered her, she was my slave, I could do
anything I liked with her. I felt exhilarated, exalted. I was
Superman.

I wasn't, you know. It took me many months before I
managed to tame the Spitfire. It took me about five years
before I was her complete master. But do allow young

innocence to have its little burst of ego, if you would be so kind. Do not let us all become hardened cynics at very short notice.

4

Operational

Hugh Kennard briefed me for my first battle climb, which was to be a climb at full throttle to over 30,000 feet, when we would indulge in a dog-fight. We would stay in the dispersal hut wearing our Mae Wests (life-jackets in case we fell into the sea) and would scramble when the duty pilot gave the order over the field telephone, and simultaneously shoot off a red Very cartridge to keep other aircraft away from the circuit. I went out and checked my Spitfire, which was still LZ-X – it nearly always was during the time I spent on No. 66 Squadron – and put my parachute on the wing-tip. The engine was warm enough for take-off, they always were, and the rudder and fore and aft trims needed adjustment. I placed my flying helmet and gauntlets all handy in the cockpit, returned and Hugh and I played dominoes. Then the telephone orderly gave us the scramble order, a red Very cartridge exploded at its zenith over the airfield, and Hugh bolted from the dispersal hut as quick as a cobra striking. I panted after him, and it immediately occurred to me that I would have to practise my sprinting, if I were to maintain the standards required in No. 66 Squadron.

Whilst I was fumbling with the safety harness, Hugh had already begun to taxi off the line. However, I caught up with him just as he was swinging his Spitfire for the take-off position, by dint of giving the Merlin a burst of throttle which nearly brought the dispersal house down. I trailed him into the air, and he rang up on the R/T.

'Yellow Two. Make sure your oxygen is set for a fast climb.'

I hastily checked and found that I had forgotten to switch on the supply.

At 10,000 feet he ordered me into close formation. I found

that I couldn't fly a Spitfire in close formation. I was like a weather vane being blown in all directions in constantly changing winds. I was making wild ecstatic leaps, practically colliding with him one moment, half a mile away the next. Hugh was a close observer, although the whole thing was obvious enough.

'Fall into loose line-astern formation,' he instructed. He didn't want to die in a mid-air collision.

It took me quite a long time to learn how to fly the Spitfire in close formation. The controls were so sensitive that I was leaping around like a frog, a frog singing against the fauns in the twilight of my inexperience. I was, of course, over-correcting, and the art of close-formation flying is entirely anticipatory. When I conquered the problem, and conquer it I had to do or be thrown off the squadron into the pit of Bomber Command, it all came so naturally. Just to put the wind up my section leader, I once tickled my wing-tip against his; he nearly had a heart attack, but I didn't – I knew the judgment within a few millimetres. But with Hugh Kennard in the lead at that moment in time, I didn't know who my sweet Aunt Fanny was. I was far from singing in the wilderness, and although I didn't take aboard alcohol I felt that a jug of wine might enliven me.

Hugh taught me a bit about the East Anglian landscape as we ascended beyond 30,000 feet. Our rate of climb had fallen to about a hundred feet a minute by now, and my oxygen system was turned on to full flow. The gauge indicating the amount of oxygen in the cylinder was falling rapidly, and Hugh's voice over the R/T was becoming thinner as we just about hit the service ceiling of the Spitfire.

'OK,' he said faintly, 'I am descending to 25,000 feet. Then we'll have a practice dog-fight.'

When diving from high altitude, medical problems arise. The sense of balance is maintained, I believe, by hair follicles somewhere in the middle ear which are highly sensitive. Fluid in the ear system tickles them up and signals are sent at the speed of light to the brain. Even motorists driving up mountain roads experience a feeling of blockage of the ears – or passengers in tube-trains as they make their slight descent underground. One had to constantly press the nostrils with the fingers, close the nose and puff into the nose to equilibrate the air pressure in the head with that in the unpressurized cockpit. One did it in the climb as well as the dive. I used to do it when driving cars, constantly. In many ways this practice became a habit. I used to do it in the international jet aircraft when I travelled a million and more miles around the world in under eighteen months, long after the war ended. It was daft to fly with a heavy cold on some occasions, and because the ear-tubes are then blocked with catarrh one could not stabilize the air pressures. This caused the most acute agony, and flying with a cold in any case simply made one's reactions in combat not sharp enough. Both my ear-drums are scarred to this day, possibly because I flew with a cold, or had to disengage, or attempt to make an attack, when diving like a bat out of hell. I could not say when I broke my ear-drums; it was not apparent at the time, but the fact came to light later when various doctors were making routine medical examinations.

At 25,000 feet, Hugh told me to fall behind his Spitfire by about a mile. Then he suddenly made a tight turn and straightened out in a head-on attack. I ducked as his aircraft passed a few feet over my head on a collision course. I immediately pulled round to keep him in sight, difficult enough to do at rarefied altitudes where the eyes have no frame of reference, but I spotted him and gave her full throttle in an attempt to get on his tail.

He weaved like a drunk, skidded and slipped, but I pressed the ciné-camera gun button as I centred my gun-sight on him. If I had pressed my gun-firing button, my bullets would have missed because I was outside effective range. He pulled round in a high gee turn, and I saw he was getting onto my tail – we had no rear-view mirrors at that time, and the single recourse was to weave the aircraft and crane the neck until it almost came off the shoulders, gazing obliquely behind in the lethal sector, about 30 degrees to the rear. I lost sight of him, and in desperation flicked the Spitfire onto its back, hauled her down into vertical dive, climbed out of it like a screaming jesus, and put her into an Immelmann turn at the top. That surely must have shaken him off my tail, I thought.

It had done no such thing. Hugh Kennard drew up to me in close formation a few seconds later.

'Form up in loose formation,' he said over the R/T. 'I am descending to join circuit and land.'

I reckon Hugh had put me in his gun-sight on half a dozen occasions, and if he had fired his guns, I would have been a dead duck thrice over. And I thought I had got the Spitfire tamed!

'When innocence is closing up his eyes!' More apt, perhaps: 'A daring pilot in extremity . . . would steer too nigh the sands to boast his wit.'

As the weeks rolled by, I began to learn the elementary principles of becoming an effective fighter pilot. But my more experienced colleagues were *not* fighter pilots, any more than I was. They had to learn the arts in the white heat of war, but the Germans *were* experienced fighter pilots. They learned these arts over the Iberian Peninsula during the Spanish Civil War, and the tactics they evolved the hard way were passed on to the squadrons, which did not participate in that campaign, by staff pilots serving with the *Lehr* Division based at Greifswald.

The RAF had no such equivalent unit until 1943, and the tactical doctrines taught at the flying schools so many years later were based essentially on Luftwaffe tactics, as recounted by British and Allied fighter pilots who had been in action against the Germans. We were better at dog-fighting than the fighter arm of the Luftwaffe, but only because both the Spitfire and Hurricane were more manoeuvrable than the Messerschmitts 109 and 110, also the Focke-Wulf 190 of the Luftwaffe. In fact, dog-fighting ability was not all that important during the war. Fighter

attacks were hit-or-miss affairs on average. Either you dived
with the sun behind you and caught him napping, or he did
that to you. I occasionally had to mix it in dog-fights with
German fighter pilots, and either I would shoot them down
or they would shoot me down, or I would lose sight of them
because their camouflage was better than mine. The reason
we were more manoeuvrable than them was because the Me-
109 had a higher wing loading than our fighters. This gave us
advantages, but they also had certain benefits. We had no
idea that the Daimler-Benz engines in the 109s were fuelled
by direct-injection methods. Our carburettors were a
definite handicap. The Germans could push down the nose
of their fighters, scream into a vertical dive, as if beginning a
bunt, and accelerate like mad away from us. When we tried
that tactic, our carburettors would flood under negative gee,
and our engines would stall momentarily – as they frequently
did – which lost us all-important seconds during the
engagement.

Again, we flew, in both training and combat, formations
which were ideal for the Hendon air pageants, whereas the
Luftwaffe flew in lethal, fluid, combat formations. Our
'pecking' attacks, on those rare occasions when Bomber
Command agreed to lend the odd formations of bombers for
inter-Command exercises, had nothing to do with anything
in particular. However, we trained as hard as we knew, and
not one of us, certainly not myself, realized that we were to
some large extent wasting our time. The staff at
Headquarters No. 12 Group, under whose aegis we came,
did not realize this, nor did the Air Officer Commanding the
Group, Leigh-Mallory – but he never learned about fighter
tactics.

A Flight at a time, we flew to the Armament Practice
Camp at Sutton Bridge, near King's Lynn, to fire our
Brownings. We shot at large squares of canvas set up on the
ground, which didn't teach us much; but it did give our
armourers some training in terms of clearing stoppages in
the guns, and getting them reloaded might quick sharp. We

aimed at drogues being towed at 100 mph, which bore little resemblance to shooting at Me-109s that would flash past on the beam at 350 mph. It certainly trained us in breaking off the attack when 15 degrees from the towing aircraft, else the tug aircraft would have gone up in flames. Our ciné-camera firing exercises were not helpful, for the cameras usually did not operate effectively, or the heating was inadequate at height and the lenses iced up. But on the occasions when the films were good enough to be displayed, that was of little use since we had neither the equipment nor the trained analysts to make much sense from the films.

However, I accumulated some experience which was to stand me in good stead, somehow or another. It certainly taught me the arts of self-survival. It must have, since I was the sole survivor from the pilots of No. 66 Squadron, apart from Sergeant Pilot Duggie Hunt, when I assumed command of the outfit in the early summer of 1941. Don't ask me how Duggie got away with it, for I couldn't say. I by no means 'got away with it' but I survived. The rest were killed, burned, more severely wounded than I was, or were posted from the Squadron, some of them destined to die with other squadrons.

After a few weeks, Billy Burton gave me a flight commander's check-out, beat me hollow in a dog-fight, but declared me operational. I had also been passed out at taking off the Spitfire and landing it at night, although I all but killed myself on my first night solo. So I was placed on the operational roster, to fly strictly as No. 2 on the section commander's wing. This meant that I had to fly interminable convoy patrols, mucking around over small coastal convoys for hours. I used to fly on about the level of the Plimsoll line of the ships, and the only enjoyment I gained was watching the merchant seamen. They often wore trousers and vests, nothing much else, and I remember one large man solemnly placing a tin bucket on the end of a mop and waving it furiously at me. Another waved a bottle of what must have been rum, and hurled it at my Spitfire, but I was in no condition to catch it and drink his health.

I always kept a safe distance away from the naval escort ships, if any, because no one had taught the Navy anything about aircraft recognition. If they could have shot straight, and they couldn't, they would have holed me on innumerable occasions. They didn't know the difference between a Heinkel 111 and a Sopwith Camel, nor did they care very much. Their theory was that any aircraft that came within range should be fired on, because a ship is more expensive than an aircraft, even if it happened to be British, and was there in their defence. Come to think of it, it seems that I normally flew convoy patrols on my own, not as a fighter section. I remember escorting a British cruiser on a few sorties; I believe it was HMS *Ajax* returning for repairs after assisting in the engagement against the German pocket-battleship, *Graf Spee*, which was scuttled in Montevideo Bay. She was a glorious sight.

There were other chores. My pilot's flying log-book indicates that I was in the squadron formation which made a ceremonial fly-past for the Duke of Gloucester when he paid a visit to Duxford. I had to stay at readiness for regular stints, at thirty minutes, fifteen, or immediate readiness. In full-moon conditions I would be at readiness throughout the night – Britain had no proper night fighter defence. It was ineffective to order day flight squadrons off at night to attempt interceptions on the occasional German bombers which used to hive over into our air space. The idea was that searchlights would cone in onto the hostile, thereby indicating the target to us, and we would swoop in at devastating speed and shoot it down. Even in full-moon conditions, one would have needed the eyesight of a witch to do anything like that. In any case, the exhausts of the Merlin were red-hot, blinding at night, and it was difficult enough to land a Spitfire at night, let alone get to within firing range.

The sort of thing that occurred, of course, can be explained. A pilot on No. 19 Squadron, our rivals at

Duxford, was ordered off on a night interception. He got to within four miles of the target, although he could not, of course, see it. Our searchlights then coned in onto his Spitfire, and for once in their lives the ack-ack guns struck the target – the wrong target. He managed to bail out, his parachute fortunately opened, and he discovered that one of his legs had been shot away. He also took note that a main artery was spurting blood from his body at such a rate that he would be dead in about a minute. Clearly he was a cool customer, and at that moment in time was not enamoured at the prospect of meeting St Peter. By good fortune he had clasped in his hand the steel wire of the rip-cord of his parachute. He made a quick decision, wrapped the steel wire round his thigh which was missing a lower leg, and tightened the noose as hard as he could. This acted as a primitive torniquet, but he hung onto it, literally for grim death.

He hit the ground with a thump, but maintained his firm grasp on the tourniquet which was his single life-line. He lay on the grass, maintaining his grip on the tourniquet, and hoped. How they found him at night God knows, I don't, but they did. His stump was eventually sliced down to size, he was given a tin leg, and then he continued to fly operationally on fighters. Perhaps he doubted but never turned his back; he marched breast forward; but I know that if I had been in his situation, I would have doubted very much whether the clouds would ever break.

Day by day I was gaining precious operational experience. One or two even less experienced pilots joined the squadron and, poor things, thought I was a highly experienced and established ace. When I disillusioned one of them, he confessed that he had only taken me to be an ace because I looked the part; and in any case, I was on the operational roster and he was a non-operational apprentice. In the event, he turned out to be the ace before he was killed in action, whereas I would hardly suggest that I ever came into the ace category.

His name was Bodie, and he was a six-footer, heavy and

strong with it. He dressed like a ragamuffin, had an upturned button-nose, a firm jaw and had been a champion heavyweight boxer at school. His sense of discipline on the ground was non-existent, but in the air, alone in the great big sky with hundreds of German aircraft all round him, his self-discipline was exemplary. He used to chase them like a hunt terrier after foxes which had gone to ground, and preferred to attack German bombers head-on. He blew up at least six in this fashion, but he by no means escaped unscathed from the 109s. He always carried a small camera in his tunic pocket and once told a farmer to photograph him standing by his Spitfire in a field in which he had belly-landed due to battle damage. He returned so often with great gashes in his aircraft through enemy machine-gun and cannon fire, but he carefully took his photographs before being carted off to the sick bay to be looked over by the doctor.

After interception a Dornier 17 he was hit by return fire, but managed to nurse his faltering engine back to Duxford. The Spitfire caught fire on his final approach to land, too low for him to bail out. Bogle – as we called him – side-slipped like fury to keep the flames away from his face, leaped out of the cockpit when his aircraft was proceeding along on the grass at over 45 mph. He was completely winded, watched the Spitfire run along with no pilot in the cockpit, suddenly wheel round on its undercarriage and head directly towards him, burning furiously as it did so. The fiery flames beat the aircraft to the punch and it collapsed onto its belly, whereupon the unused ammunition shot merrily away from the heat, and seemed to be pointing straight at the aircraft's erstwhile pilot. He recovered from the shock in about five minutes, and dived into an enormous breakfast of ham and eggs – he was a hearty eater.

Bodie was posted from No. 66 Squadron in October 1940 after I had assumed command of his flight. In the end I destroyed more German aircraft than he did in his short life-span. But if anyone thinks I was an ace when compared with Bodie, as Reichsmarschall Goering said, before a famous

non-event which proved him to be wrong, 'Call me Meier.'
But call Bodie a true ace, 1940 vintage.

Billy Burton was leading my section on an interception
scramble when radar, or RDF as it was called in those days,
put him on course and we intercepted a Junkers 88 far out
over the North Sea. He led the attack but opened fire far out
of range; I thought I was just about within range, but I
wasn't because the Ju-88 escaped and ran for Holland. This
was a very fast-flying, versatile bomber, which was used as
an effective night fighter later in the war. I thought I saw
white smoke issuing from one of the engines after my attack,
but it probably came from the rear-gunner's cigar, not from
the engine. Still, I had at least fired my guns, more in
desperation than in anger.

Then on another interception, under the leadership of the
skilful and worthy Flight-Sergeant Pilot Cameron, who used
to watch the little people suckle badgers in Ireland as a
youth, we bust open a Dornier 17. (' 'Tis Ireland gives
England her soldiers, her generals too.') But I was by now
getting the feeling that I was a Phoebus Apollo turning
fasting friar. Cameron went in first on a high quarter attack,
fired his guns and I never saw him again until I landed back
at Duxford. He lost sight of the bomber after his attack, all
too easy to do. I shot the rear gunner in the eye according to
my tracer bullets, except I didn't. Pickering, the No. 3 in the
Section, went in last while I hovered above, having used up
all my ammunition in my attack. He opened fire at close
range, and vanished. I watched the Dornier, which shot
black smoke from one engine, begin to spiral down. It
suddenly went into a spin and I prognosticated that the
curtains had now been drawn over the German scenario. I
was plumb right.

This flying corpse spun down, and I followed it almost to
sea level, in its wake. (Holy Mary, as the Irish priest
pronounced, all I want is to be present at me own wake.) It
dived into the sea and I circled the spot, watched oil spewing

to the surface, which was followed by little yellow objects –
probably life-saving dinghies for the hapless aircrew. It was
all a bit sickening. *Absence abominable absinthe de la guerre.*
But I don't know about that, for they got Pickering.

Pickles, as we called him, was slightly taller than average,
thin as a broomstick, with sunken cheeks and with very
sharp, but slightly protruding eyes. He had been a champion
sprinter at school, for his long legs could shove his thin body
along quicker than a rat attempting to get away from the
deadly jaws of a Staffordshire bull-terrier. (The rats were
dead unlucky; a Staffordshire still holds the record for the
sport of rat-killing.) He was always in and out of hospital for
reasons to do with battle damage to his body. I think he
rather enjoyed it, because more often than not, in 1940–41,
many nurses were most attractive young ladies. I savoured
the experience only once, but I dearly wished that I could
hang around Guy's for a couple of years.

The gallant, if haphazard, Pickles got a few German
bullets in his glycol tank during his close-range attack,
mainly because I had not, as I thought I had, killed the rear
gunner. Naturally his engine seized up over the sea, but he
managed to belly-land near a manned lightship. The Spitfire
scooped up sea water with its large radiator and other
configurations on the fuselage, and Pickles nose-dived into
the sea to such a depth that the water turned colour from
green to black. He was deeper than full fathom five when he
burst from his cockpit, but somehow the crew of the
lightship managed to drag him out and apply artificial
respiration.

The Navy sent along an MTB to collect him, whereupon
the Luftwaffe decided to bomb Chatham as the boat hove to.
Which excited Pickles almost as much as the nurses in the
naval hospital at Greenwich when they got him there. But he
arrived back at No. 66 Squadron within a week. We thought
he was a ghost. We had posted him as killed in action. In the
end he was killed on active service.

Little did I dream that I should see such disasters in a

nation of gallant men. But there were far more disasters than those already described ahead of me.

Then came Dunkirk.

5

Dunkirk and After

I had been on the squadron for something over a month when Rupert Leigh arrived from the operations room and called a conference with his flight commanders. Billy Burton, as previously related, was commanding B Flight, the flight wherein I was installed. In command of A Flight was Ken Gillies, short, dark hair, immaculate in his dress, with rabbity teeth and an almost constant grin on his face. One had one's loyalties, but secretly I preferred Ken Gillies to Billy Burton. Ken was an exceptional fighter pilot by the standards of the day and, with due respect to Billy's memory, I would never have placed him within that select category. Ken had proved himself as the best shot at the drogue in the whole of Fighter Command, just for starters. Billy couldn't shoot straight – although he learned those arts some time after he left No. 66 Squadron, mainly against ground targets. Before he was killed in the North African campaign, Billy had sewn on his tunic the DSO, DFC and bar, but he did not destroy a German aircraft during the Battle of Britain. Ken Gillies shot down three German bombers, with two others shared before he was killed in action early in October; yet he was awarded no decoration whatsoever, even though he was one of the most gallant pilots I ever served with. Courage is almost a contradiction in terms. The British system of awarding decorations for gallantry is, and usually was, ludicrous.

Apart from his extreme charm and likeableness, Ken was a great asset to the squadron both professionally and socially. He could play the piano with flair, even though he was self-taught, even though he could not read music. Bawdy RAF ballads came as easily to him as Chopin's nocturnes. Music is important to airmen. We lived in a world of music on the ground; there was merely the murmuring of phantoms in the air. Ken assisted us by his ability to play the hit tunes of the day. Cole Porter, Irving Berlin, Hoagy Carmichael were our favourite composers. *The Things You Are*, *Stardust* and, above all, *Blue Orchids* were our beloved melodies. I would give away Carrickfergus, assuming that I owned it, for a true, original record of *Blue Orchids*.

So there was Ken, brilliant fighter pilot and pianist one day, dust to dust not long afterwards. Ashes to ashes, dust to dust, if the good Lord don't get you, then the devil must, as we used to say in the RAF. We also used to say, when we were dying or thought we were, to hell with everybody except the stretcher-bearers.

It was all terribly hush-hush after the secret confab. between our top brass. All we pilots and bog-rats were told was to be at readiness at first light the next day, and that the squadron would be taking off for an unknown destination. We were likely to be away for some time. Twelve aircraft would be detailed for take-off, and the remainder would be kept at thirty minutes' readiness in case reinforcements were required. The senior NCOs were ordered to change the crystals on the VHF radios according to the instructions, and to work the airmen all through the night to get every Spitfire serviceable, within the bounds of prudence. The Squadron Adjutant was ordered to signal every pilot and airman who were lucky enough to be on leave, and instruct them to return to Duxford immediately. Available pilots were to cram their small kit into the cockpits ahead of take-off. That was a bit of a laugh. All you could place in the cockpit of a Spitfire was a sponge-bag, containing a toothbrush and little else. (It was, in fact, possible to lay a small suitcase in the ammunition bays in the wings, provided the bays were empty. But there was no question of that possibility, since all the guns were to be armed up to the gills, with de Wilde incendiary bullets, tracer and armour-piercing; in short, the whole of our puny armament.)

Twelve of us took off at dawn the next day. I always

carried a map stuffed into one of my flying boots, and it was not too difficult to identify where we were when we joined circuit to land. It was Martlesham Heath, close to the Suffolk coast, and there were Spitfires everywhere, dispersed around the airfield with more squadrons coming in to land behind us. Somehow No. 66 Squadron slotted into that area on the airfield allocated to us. A small part of our NCOs and airmen had driven during the night to Martlesham to keep an eye on our aircraft, and they soon identified us from the letters LZ blazoned on our Spitfires.

'Cor bleeding 'ell,' Corporal Kelly said to me as I climbed out of my cockpit. 'You've never seen such a shambles as we've got 'ere.'

He was plumb right.

There were nothing like sufficient petrol bowsers available to top up our fuel tanks, very few station maintenance personnel there to assist our own fitters and riggers in inspecting the aircraft. We left our parachutes in the cockpits, there was nowhere else to put them; but someone had rigged up a small marquee where we could sit down and look at the maps. Agreed, this was a strictly improvised operation ordered at very short notice, and although our airmen extemporized to the best of their ability, the pilots had to muck into the mêlée. When a bowser happened to arrive on the squadron scene, I flagged the driver down, grabbed a screwdriver, undid the caps on the fuel tanks of my Spitfire and held the hose, directed it into the orifices of the tanks while the driver set the petrol pumps going on the tanker. At the end of the operation, although splattered with petrol, LZ-X was ready to roll on demand.

In the meantime Rupert Leigh had gone to the operations room to be briefed on the plan – some 'plan'! He returned and gave us his report. What was left of the British Army in France was to be evacuated via Dunkirk in every sort of vessel imaginable, ranging from private yachts, cross-Channel paddle-steamers, to naval destroyers. We were to provide air cover over the evacuation to fend off attacks on the amphibious forces by the Luftwaffe. Fair enough. But Rupert continued with his monologue of misery and futility. Dunkirk was quite a long flight for us in our Spitfires, essentially short-range interceptor fighters, so with luck we would be able to hang around over Dunkirk for a maximum of only three-quarters of an hour. When we had to return, or run out of petrol, further units would relieve us and maintain air cover.

We were to assemble in wings of up to four squadrons before setting forth to Dunkirk, and we had never operated so much as a wing of two squadrons in training. In 1940, due to the antiquated tactical handbooks, no squadron commander could control his squadron in warm combat conditions, so who could have the slightest prospect of maintaining tactical command over large wings? Worse, we were to operate at about 30,000 feet, acting as high cover over other formations at 20,000 feet. But cloud conditions were such at the time that the squadrons below us would be obliterated from our sight by thick layers of clouds. Even worse, due to the totally inadequate logistics support on the airfield, it was only with the greatest difficulty that a single squadron could be serviced after landing. The arrival back of four squadrons within the same time-bracket, while other wings had taken off to relieve us, automatically meant chaos, lunacy, a farrago, bedlam, confusion, disarray, hotchpotch, perplexity and an imbroglio. All this was obvious to me, a mere bog-rat entering my twentieth year.

The obvious plan would have been to dispatch individual squadrons the moment their Spitfires had been declared serviceable, wave after wave after wave. They should have been detailed to provide aircraft cover over Dunkirk and its environs at a mean altitude of 10,000 feet, or below cloud base. Squadron commanders should have been ordered to concentrate on the bombers, and ward off any attacks by the comparatively few German fighters available. (The main Luftwaffe force had been detailed to attack the retreating French armies around the Somme.) In the event, No. 66

Squadron, for example, was hardly ever in a position to give the BEF any worthwhile air cover. In order to illustrate the theme, I give below extracts from a written account by one of our pilots. This came about because later in 1940, I asked a number of pilots to write their personal recollections of their combat experience, and I have retained those memoirs:

We were ordered to take off at dawn and to be at 27,000 feet over Dunkirk . . . Having flown for some twenty minutes, I noted that my oxygen supply was draining away much too quickly, and I appreciated that there must be a leak in the system. I elected to carry on until the gauge showed danger level. I set the system to give me oxygen at a level of 10,000 feet, but when we passed 20,000 feet I began to feel faint. Perforce, I had to give myself more oxygen, but the gauge was showing that the needle would enter the red area very soon. When we arrived over Dunkirk, my eyes were almost fully concentrated on checking my oxygen supply and I was about to inform my squadron commander that I would have to break formation and return to base, when someone sighted German aircraft below. The squadron went into a steep dive, thus solving my problem.

At about 12,000 feet I saw German bombers, He-111s and Do-17s flying over Dunkirk, which was a change, for during our sweeps during the last three days we had seen nothing of the enemy. My windshield quickly became iced up as we dived, and no sooner had I wiped the ice away than it formed again. I managed to get a bead on a bomber, pressed the firing button, and I think I saw bullet-strikes on its fuselage. I began to climb, at which moment I spotted an Me-109 circling above. I turned hard to port and he disappeared. Then suddenly plumes of white smoke issued from my exhausts, and I thought I had been hit by German or French flak. Black smoke and oil fumes enveloped me from under my feet, blotting out everything and suffocating me.

After a struggle, I managed to heave open the cockpit canopy which cleared the fumes away and brought me back to my senses. I switched off the magnetos in case the engine exploded, undid my safety-harness, removed the flying helmet and prepared to bail out. At which moment, I saw an Me-109, probably the same one as before, coming up behind me, which put me right on the spot. I made a sharp diving turn into a huge pall of smoke issuing from a bombed oil refinery, and when I emerged into the sunshine, Fritz had vanished. I quickly bailed out at about 2,000 feet, and hurt my back on landing. British troops picked me up for I was incapable of moving, having severely injured my back. I was ferried back to Harwich and stayed in hospital for a month before being released to return to No. 66 Squadron.

That account gives away a number of secrets. It indicates that we were flying far too high to be effective. It also shows that the type of formation in which we used to fly was ineffective, which was not Rupert's fault since it was laid down as standard operational procedure in the tactical handbooks. The fact that the pilot above became separated also illustrates that squadron commanders in 1940 could not handle their squadrons as tactical entities, because of the antiquated formations flown. Certainly in my case, I almost invariably became engaged in combat, after the initial squadron attack, when on my own.

Rupert Leigh was ordered, shortly after Dunkirk, to move No. 66 Squadron from Duxford to Horsham St Faith, near Norwich – why, I simply couldn't say; a quite unnecessary and costly operation in my view. Douglas Badar had flown his Canadian Hurricane squadron to Duxford during the retreat from France, and I seem to remember that half the aircraft landed upwind, the right direction, and the other half downwind, the wrong direction. If this was in fact an hallucination, I still laugh my head off in my dreams of several Hurricanes colliding head-on on landing. Douglas was a good guy, full of guts, and despite his tin legs he played squash pretty well, and his Canadians taught him the arts of baseball.

Horsham was in the process of being built, although the runways were finished. The squadron officers had their rooms in the almost completed sergeants' mess, the senior NCOs slept in a barrack block and the airmen were given equally primitive accommodation in further barrack blocks. I don't think any of us minded much about the conditions. Close at hand was the city of Norwich, a splendid place before the Luftwaffe bombed it in a Baedeker raid. Nearby lay the Broads where one could hire boats or punts when off duty, during the gorgeous early summer of 1940. Peter Studd and I found a first-class restaurant and would gorge ourselves with good-quality food and wine. The Norwich girls were splendid, but I hardly so much as laid a finger on any one of them. The squadron routine was protection of convoys, and stand-by for interception scrambles. We stayed at Horsham for only a fortnight, and were then moved to Coltishall, a few miles away.

During the couple of years I was a member of No. 66 Squadron, we moved on nine occasions – on a 'permanent' basis – within nine months. We re-deployed to many other stations on a temporary basis, in support of various weirdly planned operations. Re-deploying a fighter squadron was quite a business. Rupert would have to write a movement order at high speed. The advance party of NCOs and airmen would journey to the new station in a small convoy of RAF trucks, and on arrival would sort out the details. If we were given a hangar, they would have to ensure that sufficient heavy equipment, such as jacks, a crane or two and suitable motor transport, was available. In our view, the squadron we relieved left things in one hell of a mess, whereas – again in our view – we tried our best to leave things nice and tidy.

The officer in charge of the advance party would, among his other duties, attempt to get reasonable rooms for the squadron officers. He would assist the Squadron Sergeant Major – we called him the Flight-Sergeant Discip. – to do likewise for the NCOs and airmen. The vanguard also transported essential tools to service the Spitfires when they came in to land in due course. Heavy items, such as starter batteries, cranes, jacks and so on, would be left for us by the departing unit. All these items had to be accounted for.

The main party would attempt to get every Spitfire possible ready for take-off, those beyond repair would be left for someone or other to send by road to maintenance units. When the squadron was good and ready on the line, the main party would ride in convoys to the nearest railway station, embark, and with great good fortune might even arrive at the new base before the Spitfires came in to land. On one occasion, through the courtesy of what is now known as British Rail, our main party was stranded on the train for forty-eight hours, which meant that the pilots had to assist the advance party to service the aircraft. The food allowance for the various parties while in transit amounted to 'that portion of the day's food allowance as yet unconsumed'. We used to make sure that they had treble that allowance, and sufficient crates of beer as was prudent to take with them.

When Rupert said 'Go', we would take off under the aegis of the rear party, who made last-minute servicing adjustments. They would remain until the billets had been cleared up, the inventory of squadron equipment accounted for, and all that. Then they would either entrain, or drive in convoy to our new base. It was a barmy system. The squadron lost operational effectiveness for forty-eight hours and more whenever we had to move station. Yet, as I said, No. 66 Squadron moved 'permanently' to nine different stations within nine months! Most of it was a waste of time and effort.

Coltishall was even nearer to the Norfolk Broads than Horsham St Faith, so I became fairly expert at navigating those inland waters – I never became expert at navigating a Spitfire; I achieved it because it seemed that all my gods *did* set their seals on my frantic endeavours. I decided to buy a car to get me to Norwich and its atmosphere of hedonism, and I found a battered Austin Seven for which I paid £5. Today, it would be worth £5,000. It did me well, until we came across a barrier on the perimeter track at Coltishall which I didn't notice. That bust the radiator, but our fitters soon fixed that up. I left the car at Coltishall, there was no alternative, when I took off in my Spitfire to fly with the squadron to Kenley, near Croydon, in August. I managed to fly back to Coltishall not long afterwards, and found that the car had been cannibalized, not that the jerks ate it. They merely removed the engine, the wheels, the gearbox and the transmission. The bodywork was in no worse condition than when I bade it a fond adieu. Farewell! An infinitely long farewell to my Austin Seven. Anyway, it had only cost me a fiver.

It was now August 1940. We were champing at the bit. It appeared that my destiny would be death from exposure to boredom. Piddling around for hours and hours over coastal convoys, with an occasional interception scramble, was not my idea of war. The guys in No. 11 Group were running into trouble with the fighter arm of the Luftwaffe while protecting convoys in the narrow Straits of Dover, hopelessly vulnerable to sudden swoops by wings of Messerschmitts 109. The Germans, of course, knew exactly where the convoys were – they could even see them through their binoculars. They knew that a couple of British fighter sections would be patrolling over them to give them air cover; they knew that it would take longer to get a couple of Hurricane squadrons scrambled in reinforcement, when bomber raids appeared on British radar screens, than to swoop in and beat the hell out of British fighters before further aircraft arrived in support.

So it was that Rupert Leigh led us down to the hot seat in No. 11 Group. It was a ferry flight to Kenley, but our guns were fully loaded. We overflew a fighter station burning from a recent Luftwaffe bombing raid, but we had slight difficulty in landing at Kenley which had also been bombed. There were burnt-out petrol bowsers everywhere, crashed Hurricanes had been swept away from the taxi-tracks, we had to dodge holes in the runway on landing – not too easy to do in the Spitfire. Later, one of our pilots landed with a splintered windshield brought about from the bullets of a German rear-gunner. He didn't notice the bomb holes because he couldn't see them. He finished up in a thirty-foot-deep crater, and no one noticed that he and his Spitfire were there for about half an hour. We took over from a squadron that had been shot to pieces, finger-ends trembling, tics working furiously on the faces of the pilots, and they got the hell out at the earliest possible moment after we landed. Rupert did not get a proper briefing, for the squadron commander who 'handed over' to him wasn't making any sense. His brief would have done us no good in any case. We were as green as sprouting tomatoes.

As a matter of historical fact, the Luftwaffe gained air supremacy over the amphibious landing area, roughly the Kent ports, on 1 September 1940. Which meant that we raw rookies from the Norfolk Broads went up just about the time when the Germans were in total command of the air. Either you were lucky or you were dead. I was lucky. On 4 September, more than half our squadron Spitfires were shot down on a single sortie. One pilot was severely burned and died a few days later. Another suffered second-degree burning – which is pretty savage treatment. Four others were wounded, and I got a small chunk of lead in my leg, my flying boot gave me certain armour plate. My port aileron didn't work, but I managed to plonk LZ-X down OK, although she would have preferred to spin in on the approach. I didn't bother to report my wound, although it was fairly painful, more the bruising than the penetration of lead into my limb. I think the lead is still there; I haven't had it X-rayed.

Billy Burton didn't come with us to Kenley. He was given command of another squadron and a replacement flight commander arrived who was ineffective. When he was shot down, Bobby Oxspring was given command of A Flight, and in October, I was made B Flight commander. Rupert Leigh was promoted out of his job in October, and Athol Forbes came along and took over command of No. 66 Squadron. I shall give my personal impressions of the Battle of Britain a few pages on, but first I would like to say something about Squadron Leader R. H. A. Leigh.

To put it mildly, Rupert Leigh was – and is – a complicated, nay complex, character. He was, and remains, my mentor. We have been friends for a very long time, through thick and through thin. He had a grain of superstition in him, and for some reason, when the seat became red-hot, he informed me that he wanted me as his No. 2, his wing-man, flying with him on his right wing. I suppose he wanted to save my life, with no thought of the possibility that I might save his. Between us we achieved both ends. He preferred not to fly on operations unless I was with him, although, of course, he did fly without me on innumerable occasions. I was his talisman, so to speak, and he was my mascot – or vice versa.

The Air Officer Commanding, 11 Group, came to see us once. He preened himself on the protective armour-plate which had been fitted behind our backs in the cockpits in June. Rupert took him by the hand and showed him his Spitfire. A German bullet had made a neat hole in his armour-plate, but fortunately had merely grazed Rupert's body. Our approach to life was casual. When the AOC, Keith Park, arrived he dropped in in a Hurricane. At least he could fly a Hurricane, which was a sight more than most of the rest of the top brass in the RAF could do. I don't think he could fly it *operationally*, however – there's flying and flying. He was wearing white flying overalls, whereas mine were black, bought in Bond Street because the RAF issue was too cumbersome. I think my choice of colour was better than his, more suited to the state of mourning we so often found ourselves in. His selection was positively gaudy. In any case, we didn't know who Keith Park was, and we didn't care very much.

The squadron adjutant took note that a strange Hurricane had taxied in to our dispersal; we were at that time based at Gravesend. Rupert was playing poker and I was beating our Intelligence Officer at chess.

'Some old geyser says he wants to see you,' Hewitt told Rupert.

'Tell him to go jump in the Thames,' Rupert replied.

Park entered our clubhouse and no one took any notice of him.

'I think I'd better introduce myself,' he said. Whereupon he pulled off his white overalls and displayed the badges of rank on his sleeve. It was all rather pathetic. He failed to impress me, I don't know about Rupert. But he did a good job, did Sir Keith Park, as he became. If anyone 'won' the Battle of Britain, it was Park, not Dowding, certainly not Leigh-Mallory.

We had adopted a casual approach to events mainly because Rupert Leigh was not over-fond of the formalities of military life. He is a product of the public school at Cheltenham, and of the RAF Officer Cadet School at Cranwell. I believe his father was a judge, and his brother a barrister. He specialized in classics when at school, but he did not conform in terms of his family tradition – although he took a course in law some time after the war when he was holding down a job in the rank of Air Commodore. He could be tough when the occasion warranted it, and it was warranted when I once hijacked his squadron commander's car – I was in a hurry and my own car wouldn't start.

He withstood the heavy casualties suffered by squadron pilots seemingly unmoved. He wasn't unmoved; he was deeply affected. He put a good face on things because he realized very well that the job of a squadron commander is to maintain the morale of squadron personnel. This he did to perfection. I am already in print in the terms that he kept the morale of every man jack in No. 66 Squadron at high level in the most desperate, impossible circumstances. This can only be achieved by personal example, and he gave us that prod. He led almost every sortie when we were based in 11 Group under his command, and on most occasions I was flying on his wing and was personal witness to his gallantry. If anyone speaks from the horse's mouth, then I do. His humorous, even fey, approach was an inspiration to us all. We couldn't have stood a martinet as our commander, and Rupert was anything but such.

When Rupert was posted from No. 66 Squadron in October 1940, I was on sick-leave having concussed myself crashing a severely damaged Spitfire. Two days after his departure, Sir Keith Park sent a signal to the Officer Commanding No. 66 Squadron. It congratulated the squadron on having shot down thirty German aircraft within a fortnight, and without loss – apart from damage to aircraft. Rupert knew nothing about that commendation until I gave him the information thirty-five years later. Yet, in that fortnight, he was in the lead on every sortie the squadron flew – and we flew up to six sorties a day. Surely, he might have been sent a copy of the congratulatory signal in his new appointment.

It was hot work at Kenley – we stayed there only a week. The airfield was not bombed while we were there, for the Luftwaffe had done their worst ahead of our arrival. But airfields, like industrial targets, need constant follow-up bombing attacks to eliminate them. Although we had nothing which could even be laughingly called a hangar, although spare parts were hard to come by, although communications were cut, we continued to operate. Sometimes when No. 66 Squadron roared into the air, the formation consisted of six or less Spitfires. Either the wrecks were being repaired, or being carted away on articulated vehicles to the factories and maintenance units. I disliked Kenley intensely, the station seemed to lack an air of tradition, a ghost train entering a long tunnel. Around, making the unlikely assumption that we could take time off, were nothing but characterless suburban shops and houses. It was a pre-war regular fighter station, badly situated both tactically and strategically. We had no time to get to know the other squadrons on the base, nor did we want to. My squadron was a self-sufficient unit, and we preferred each other's company to that of strangers. There was always rivalry, indeed jealousy, between fighter squadrons, which wasn't all to the bad. There was intense rivalry between the two flights in No. 66 Squadron, but it was friendly, scoffing, rivalry, a kind of desire to show A Flight that we in B Flight were pre-eminent. No harm done; it sharpened our mutual, affectionate relationship. It gave the squadron a keener cutting edge.

Whereas we had had to withstand only a few losses among our pilots when paddling around in Cambridgeshire and Norfolk, now we had to become used to greeting many newly joined pilots. Some came from other squadrons, for various reasons – one arrived when his squadron had been bombed on take-off and his unit was more or less written off, certainly decimated. Others came from nowhere and went to heaven or hell, or to limbo. Some we liked, some we didn't like. Either they were possessed of, or managed to attain, the peculiar style which we preferred, or they weren't. Effectiveness of assertion is the alpha and omega of style.

Presence is something quite different; a fighter squadron can have its style, but only individuals can be assessed in terms of presence. There are many meanings applicable to the word 'presence', but in the sense I refer to it the lexicographers – or those working in 1579 – translated it as 'Demeanour, aspect, or carriage of a person'. But in the case, for example, of Peter Studd, my meaning of the expression is that he made the room light up, without the need of electricity, when he entered it. The all-essential quality of leadership over men who are having a hard time in battle is not intellect – although that helps. It is presence, and it doesn't matter a damn whether you are short or tall, or malformed or whatever, in order to exude presence.

Rupert Leigh was possessed of presence, dignity and humour. Accordingly, we responded in action in the manner he preferred. Curiously, a good broadcasting voice is of the utmost importance if one is ever to be a first-rate fighter leader. One of Rupert's outstanding qualities is his cultured, quiet voice. Whereas we could see the Spitfires of our colleagues in the squadron when in flight, we could hardly recognize the pilots with flying helmets on their heads, oxygen masks, and all the trappings. When it became my turn to take the lead, I was always most careful when I gave orders over the R/T. The slightest hint of jitters in the vocal transmissions indicates to your squadron pilots that you are terrified out of your mind. A kind of mob-hysteria could then so easily set in, and the squadron would disperse in a great swooping dive, and fly away from the action. No. 66 Squadron never did that.

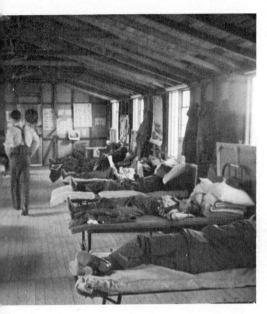

Pilots' hut, B Flight, Duxford, May 1940.

Bodie, with a cannon shell through his engine cowling. (You should have seen what happened to his opponent!)

One of my many
Spitfires annotated
LZX. (This one
burst into flame as
it buried itself deep
in the Sussex soil.)

Ken Gillies,
exceptional fighter
pilot, killed in
action October
1940. RIP.

Bobby Oxspring, my friend and colleague. Gravesend, 1940.

Pookie aboard Spitfire Mk II, 1941.

Pickering, who left No 66 squadron in Spring 1941 to train embryo fighter pilots. He was killed on active service when a trainee pilot collided with his Spitfire. RIP.

My 2-litre Lagonda in wartime trim. Biggin Hill, 1940.

Red Section, 15 minutes available, 1941. *Centre:* Flight Sergeant Kelly.

'Long-range' Spitfires Mk II taking off, Perranporth 1941. Note extra fuel tank under port wing.

Left to right: Dizzy, Beau, and Athol with Pookie.

Author piloting Spitfire Mk XXI contraprop 1945. (If we'd had them in 1940, the Luftwaffe would have been massacred in a very few days.)

Author in Spitfire Mk XXI, pressurised cockpit, gyro gun-sight, four cannon and all mod cons, 1945.

The author making the first experiment in laying chemical smoke. Meteor Mk IV, Tangmere 1950.

6

The Battle for Kent

As the frenzy, popularly known as the Battle of Britain, was reaching its climax, Rupert was, all of a sudden, ordered to re-deploy his squadron from Kenley to Gravesend – let's say thirty miles as the crow flies. The cumbersome movement operation began and in due course – having taken off on an interception scramble in order to kill two birds with one stone – we landed at the small grass airfield.

Gravesend was immensely to our liking. It was a pre-war airport, not a regular fighter station, and it lacked all the pretence which goes with the latter. Our pilots' dispersal room was the old clubhouse, furnished with not uncomfortable armchairs, and integral to its design was a bar. (We didn't need Dutch courage, but it was useful to have brandy available if one landed with a bullet-hole in a limb.) Behind the room were the kitchens and so on, and in the room was a microphone intended to relay the scramble order around the airfield. We immediately got hold of a gramophone and our favourite records, and installed them within easy reach of the microphone. From dawn to dusk our kind of music sighed round the airport, breaking our neighbours' eardrums – assuming they hadn't been already broken by the roar of the Merlins being run up, or on take-off; but we also used the microphone for the scramble order, to allow the mechanics time to get the engines started ahead of our sprint to the Spitfires.

The 'hot-line' was merely a field telephone. To contact the controller our telephone orderly would turn a handle, and a bell would ring at the Sector Operations Room at Biggin Hill, under whose aegis we lay. How he in return made our telephone ring, I don't know and I don't care. I hated controllers; they were the people who gave us the scramble

order. They gave such orders all too frequently for my liking.
Our ground crews had their offices and rest rooms in
wooden sheds nearby. We all had our billets not far from the
Spitfires, and the airmen's dining rooms, etc., were all nice
and handy. It was a cosy set-up and we liked being there.
Apart from a special flight consisting of a few Hurricanes
Mk 2, we were the only squadron based there. Rupert was
the 'Camp Commandant', officer in charge of the station,
not that he worried too much about inspecting the
lavatories, he left that sort of chore to Pat Hewitt, the
squadron adjutant. He was kept rather busy leading
the squadron in the air.

We had no hangars, but there were aircraft sheds, useful
for storing items of equipment. When I wandered into a shed
I saw for the first time a de Havilland Comet, a little twin-
engine monoplane which broke many world records flying
to places like Australia. It was a gorgeous toy, brain-child of
Sir Geoffrey de Havilland, and from its simple and clean
design he went on to produce the mighty, ubiquitous
Mosquito – night fighter, light bomber, coastal strike
aircraft, escort fighter, photo-reconnaissance aircraft –
which flew so high and so fast that German day fighters
could hardly intercept it. The Air Staff didn't want it,
probably because the fuselage was made of plywood, but it
was forced on them and became the most successful multi-
role aircraft in the war.

When we had time to explore the environs around the
airfield, which was normally when the squadron was stood
down at nightfall, there was a pub near the waterfront in the
town of Gravesend with a bar made of solid pewter about
thirty feet in length. It was battered from continual usage,
but the pewter would be worth many tens of thousands of
pounds today. The airfield stood high above the town, and I
expect the population got used to our noisy Merlins revving
up at strange hours.

Farther afield was Chatham and its Empire Theatre,
where I stole my flying scarf from a seven veil dancer, or

stripper – except that she didn't want to strip off everything and I had to do that for her. A number of dignitaries came to visit us, presumably to assist in giving us the Last Sacraments. One such was George, Duke of Kent, a most engaging and sophisticated man with a great sense of humour. He looked at my scarf enviously, and his covetousness grew apace when he bent his head and sniffed it. It smelt of cheap scent and perspiration, and it had recently been removed from its role of guardian of the sexual parts of a music-hall dancer. He asked me if I would give it to him as a souvenir, but I firmly refused. It was a good scarf and eased the chafing of my neck, as I turned my head so outrageously to watch for the Germans coming up behind that I nearly broke my spinal cord.

The Secretary of State for Air, Sir Archibald Sinclair, came to see us, and I put up a black. Sir Archibald obviously knew very little about aeroplanes which was probably why he was given his political appointment. But it seemed to me that his private detective knew quite a lot about aeroplanes. It must have been his detective because he wore a black homburg hat and followed closely behind the Secretary of State.

'A policeman's lot is not supposed to be a happy one,' I said. 'Are you enjoying accompanying half-baked politicians all round the place?'

'Oh yes,' he replied. 'I find the whole thing most interesting.'

Thirty years later, I elucidated that the 'detective' was Parliamentary Under Secretary of State for Air. He is now Lord Balfour of Inchrye, a First World War air ace to boot. He really enjoyed pulling my leg.

Officially the Battle of Britain began on 10 July and ended on 31 October. As far as I am concerned, it lasted for me for the whole period we were based in 11 Group – August 1940– February 1941. Our saddest loss was Ken Gillies. It seems that he was shot down by the rear gunner of a Heinkel 111 and fell into the sea. When he did not return, Rupert posted him as missing, and three weeks later his body was washed out of the Thames, but his indestructible identity tag showed that he had once been Ken. Many pilots arrived and vanished so quickly that I hardly had time to get to know them. One such was Pilot Officer Reilly, a Canadian, with fair curly hair, who spoke with a quiet drawl, and chewed gum. Both he and Ken were killed in October.

My first real hand-shake with death came on 11 October, although we had met before that. But perhaps the most vivid way to illustrate my own experiences during the Battle of Britain would be to take a few extracts from side-notes scrawled in my pilot's flying log-book, 1940 edition. I've got a number of log-books covering my career as a fighter-pilot, test-pilot, photo reconnaissance-pilot, light bomber-pilot, and a few more roles than just those. But my favourite is the 1940 edition, showing my gradual increase in pilot experience, together with notes on my successes and failures, scribbled in schoolboy writing:

4 September: Attacked four Heinkels heavily escorted by Me-109s. Got within range, saw black smoke, then departed in a hurry.

5 September: To Hawkinge and return. [Perhaps I should explain that casual note. Volunteers were called for and I put my hand up. It was a secret mission. All we were told was that we should arrive at the small airfield at Hawkinge, just behind Folkestone, before dawn broke the next morning. Led by Bobby Oxspring, three Spitfires took off before first light, and none of us knew what the hell it was all about. We covered a dilapidated Anson as it wearily climbed to 10,000 feet over Calais, spotting for long-range British artillery. It took the Luftwaffe an hour to react, then I saw a gaggle of German fighters climbing to intercept us. I ordered the pilot of the Anson to beat it for home; he exceeded the design limits of his aircraft as he dived to safety. That was the longest hour of my life.]

5 September: Jumped by 109s as I took a bead on another.

I hit him but they got me. One of my ailerons was shot away, a bullet punctured my leg, there were a dozen bullet-holes in my Spitfire. It was write-off, but I landed it OK.

9 September: Attacked 215s [presumably meaning Dorniers]. I shot down 109s (how many?). Shot down Heinkel 111, saw crew captured by Home Guard.

11 September: Attacked mass formation of bombers. One He-111 forced down, saw it crash land.

11 September: Jumped by 109s. Managed to escape.

11 September: Met a Heinkel, already crippled. Forced it down, saw it crash-land.

15 September: Forced down two bombers.

15 September: Attacked large bomber formation over London. Shot down one Heinkel and one Dornier, both on fire.

16 September: Interception patrol at 30,000 ft. No breakfast. Ugh!

19 September: Squadron patrol at 30,000 ft. Shot down one Me-109.

25 September: Lone weather patrol over English Channel. Saw Calais.

27 September: Ran into twenty Me-110s. Rather stupidly attacked head-on. [These twin-engine fighters had heavy forward-firing cannon and machine-guns.] No strikes seen. Learned later that other squadrons shot down the lot.

30 September: Attacked an Me-109. After first squirt he leaked glycol. Second squirt, bits fell off. Third squirt, distinctive tail struts fell off. Black smoke issued. Left him in order to gain combat altitude.

30 September: Jumped by 109s. Didn't get a chance to fire, but got back to base OK.

5 October: Considerable dog-fights with Me-109s. Felt bloody awful – had a heavy cold.

11 October: Squirted at Me-109 at extreme range. Saw glycol pour out, then black smoke. It simply fell out of the air. I was hit by British ack-ack returning from mid-Channel. Oil from Merlin covered my windshield. Glided to Hawkinge. Could only see with head stuck out of the cockpit. Landed wheels down. Brakes wouldn't work. Hit barbed wire at 60 mph, severely concussed. Total loss of memory for a week. [This deserves some explanation. The guns of the Army Ack-Ack Command were hopelessly inadequate, in terms of gun-aiming, type of shell used, and fuses timed to explode at a certain height. The aircraft recognition of the gunner was poor, so the Five-Thousand-Feet Rule was brought in, which was abject nonsense. Because aircraft recognition hardly existed, it was decided between Ack-Ack Command and Fighter Command Headquarters – who should have known something about things but didn't – that *any* aircraft crossing the English coast, either on entry of flying towards the Continent, were to be fired on. At great height it is impossible to say whether you are ahead of the coast, over the coastline, or to seaward. They hadn't thought of that. In any case, was I going to turn back just because I was over the coast when I was catching up with a gaggle of Germans! I should think that my Spitfire was about the only target our ack-ack managed to shoot down in 1940 . . .]

24 October: Squirted an Me-109 at 32,000 ft, extreme range. Saw black smoke from its engine. Saw it spin down.

26 October: Landed at Luton to ask where I was. Hadn't got the first idea.

30 October: Squadron moved to West Malling.

8 November: Squadron moved to Biggin Hill.

11 November: Became involved with 50 Me-109s. Got the hell out.

14 November: Squadron engaged 40 Junkers 87 attacking Dover, covered by Me-109s. Made many attacks from all angles. Hits on two. Black smoke poured from another, couldn't wait to watch it crash. Used up all my ammunition on the fourth. Watched him crash into the sea, tremendous splash. It was burning like hell when it went in. [*Note:* That night the Luftwaffe made a heavy raid on Coventry. Two-thirds of war production in the area was temporarily lost. The fourteenth-century cathedral was ruined. In which context, despite the massive raids on that city, Cologne cathedral escaped unscathed. It is said that the priests offered special prayers for its salvation; if so, the power of Teutonic prayer must have been of a higher grade than that of the priests serving Coventry's cathedral.]

28 November: Leading B Flight on interception course. My number four, Sergeant Wilcox, collided with me. Saw him go down minus a tail fin. Bailed out. Landed near East Grinstead having just curled out of the way of high-tension electricity cables. Hung up a tree. Home Guard thought about shooting me. Told them to go to hell. Wilcox killed – fortunately, or I would have shot him in any case.

30 November: Landed after an interception patrol with only two gallons of petrol in the tanks. [Bobby Oxspring was leading the flight, and fog descended on our way back. Only Bobby could have found his way back – it was by instinct, not navigation. Had I been in the lead I would have diverted the flight if possible, or ordered the pilots to climb high enough to bail out. Not Bobby! He got us back with seconds to spare.]

7 December: Reconnaissance patrol. Thick fog clamped down. Forced landed at Gravesend (I was obviously lucky to get away with that one).

11December: Reconnaissance patrol. One Messerschmitt 109 shot down.

7 February 1941: Balloon chase. Two balloons shot down. [Two barrage balloons broke their moorings and floated towards France. I can't think why they should not have been allowed to drop to earth at somewhere like Paris, it would have done no harm to anybody. However, I was ordered to shoot them down over mid-Channel. I wondered whether they would blow up in my face as my explosive bullets struck, but they didn't. They collapsed like an old lady suffering from dropsy who had decided to give up the ghost. It was particularly unimpressive.]

13 February: Weather test. Cloud base 40 feet, no hope of penetrating. Returned to base. [No international airline today would authorize a pilot to take off if the cloud base was 40 feet! From the ground I told them the cloud base was 40 feet. They didn't believe me – they told me to take off and prove it. Where left you Chrononhotonthologos?]

14 February: Jumped by Messerschmitts 109, Wing formation by Germans. Wounded in right arm. Crashed at Biggin Hill.

The incidents on 11 December and 14 February deserve more detailed accounts. And *en passant*, I stress that these side-notes in my pilot's flying log-book are merely extracts from the other notes which give a more comprehensive picture of events:

11 December: Reconnaissance patrol. One Messerschmitt 109 shot down.

This was a minor classic interception. No. 66 Squadron was patrolling and had gained height to about 20,000 feet somewhere over East Grinstead with Athol Forbes in the lead. I was leader of Yellow section flying near his starboard wing. The Biggin Hill Controller rang up on the R/T. 'Fibus Leader,' he broadcast, 'there is a bandit approaching Chatham, estimated course 150 degrees, estimated height 10,000 feet. Request you intercept.'

Athol wasn't prepared to dive the whole squadron down to intercept a single German aircraft. Instead, he broadcast: 'Yellow Leader break formation and intercept bandit.' I wheeled my section to starboard, dived towards Chatham and instructed the two pilots accompanying me to form section line-astern, a flexible combat formation. It is difficult to see a black spot, i.e. a single German aircraft, in the infinite blue of the skies. So I requested the controller over the R/T to instruct his ack-ack liaison officer to order the anti-aircraft artillery barrage to fire at the bandit. I knew they hadn't a hope of shooting it down – if they had I could have returned to base and gone to bed. But one can hardly fail to see ack-ack shell bursts, whereas a black spot before the eyes could be a bandit, or part of the results of a hangover from the night before. The ground gunners acted promptly, and I bust the seal on my throttle segment when I saw the burst of shell-fire. We closed range rapidly and I saw a spot which soon materialized in the form of a lone Me-109, probably performing a quick reconnaissance to assist the raid which the German bombers had planned for that night.

I then instructed the guns to cease fire, and told the two pilots in my section to attack in turn after me. I closed range to 250 yards at an angle off of about fifteen degrees, laid off the requisite deflection in my gun-sight, pressed my firing button and lo and behold! The engine of the Messerschmitt immediately exploded in flames, the pilot hastily bailed out, and we saw his parachute open with a jerk.

'I'm going to beat the bastard up,' I said over the R/T to my section. 'Don't collide with him, but make it look as if you intend to.'

I flew ten feet below the dangling pilot at well over 400 mph, and saw his parachute swing like fury from my slip-stream. The other two did likewise. He might have died from a heart attack, but that didn't worry me too much – he had plenty of height for his parachute to regain its poise. Then I asked the controller to vector me back to my squadron. We intercepted No. 66 Squadron quite neatly, and regained battle formation under Athol's leadership. I knew I had shot the Me-109 down with a very short burst, so on landing I asked the armourers to be careful to count the bullets fired. They did. It had needed less than a half-second burst to get him. I fired only twenty rounds per gun, 160 bullets in all. Good shooting, possibly one for the *Guinness Book of Records*.

Thirty-five years later, a man telephoned me and told me

that his team of modern archaeologists had dug up an Me-109 which crashed on 11 December 1940 somewhere south of Chatham, at such-and-such time; and that I had shot it down. I told him not to be so silly. How could he possibly identify a wreck dug out from thirty feet under the ground with me?

'Have a look in your log-book,' he replied.

I did. And he was plumb right! Clever chaps, these diggers. They work things out in such detail as to confuse even people like Sherlock Holmes.

14 February: Jumped by Messerschmitts 109, Wing formation by Germans. Wounded in right arm. Crashed at Biggin Hill.

The background to that incident is as follows. After about 15 September 1940, the Luftwaffe's bombers were concentrated on night attacks on London. They bombed the city for fifty-five nights, either slightly or most damagingly. I haven't researched the number of monuments which were destroyed or damaged, but I believe that more than twenty exquisite Wren churches no longer exist. I know that St Paul's Cathedral was hit; and so was Buckingham Palace on a day raid. But the fighter arm of the Luftwaffe also attacked London by day, using Me-109s fitted with bombs, and when they were dropped at random on London, the Messerschmitts then became fighters in their own right, not fighter-bombers; so one had to watch one's step. In any case, to us they presented a most difficult problem, for they could gain altitude over occupied France, head for London at great height and at full speed, and then release their bombs over the sprawling mass of our capital city.

Our best tactic in reply was to form standing patrols, covering lines such as Maidstone to Dover at combat altitude. Indeed, because of our tactics, we intercepted the Stuka raid on Dover on 14 November just as the Germans arrived over the target. We wouldn't have had a hope if we had relied on a scramble response based on radar and Royal Observer Corps reports – the reporting took far too long to be effective when considering coastal targets. But on 14 February, we were scrambled to intercept a force of Me-109s; the controller realized they were German fighters because of the speed of flight indicated by the radars. I was leading No. 66 Squadron and I was highly suspicious of the controller, whose voice I recognized over the R/T, and who to my mind was not good at his job. Nevertheless I followed his instructions, instead of using my own nous, and put the squadron into close formation to penetrate a layer of cloud base about 10,000 feet and approximately 3,000 feet thick. I ordered the squadron to adopt battle formation as we cleared the cloud, and the sun was dead ahead, blindingly so. Before you could say 'President Jimmy Carter' fifty Me-109s descended on us like eagles to lambs. (We were clearly silhouetted, with the background of cloud below us, and the blinding sun was behind them, giving them the total advantage.)

Someone spotted them diving like hawks, but my eyes were not yet re-focused from flying on instruments in order to lead the squadron through the cloud. He shouted over the R/T, 'Fibus Squadron Break!' We all hauled round, but I was a few seconds too late. My Spitfire shuddered as it was struck by a minor cannonade of high explosive, armour-piercing and other forms of German missiles. My right arm was flung upwards through enormous forces as a bullet penetrated my bicep and grazed my ribs as it passed through the arm and close to the body. My knuckles of the right hand were severely bruised as they struck the cockpit canopy like an ascending thunderbolt through the force of the bullet. This *kshatriya*, me, I thought to myself, is a dead duck. Then the initial shock was over, and I pulled myself together. He was just another bloody German who was lucky enough to get in the first punch. In all rationality, he had been overtaking me so fast that *he* would be the sitting duck, not me.

I hastily took control of the Spitfire with my left hand, my right arm was hanging down limply spouting blood. I saw him; he had a big, dirty, yellow nose acting as a cowl for the engine of his Messerschmitt 109. He also had two cannon projecting from his wings, whereas I had merely eight light Browning machine-guns. I jacked her round – it was like trying to write with your left hand, not your right. I got on his tail, closed to 250 yards, pressed the firing button, and smiled at the prospect of seeing him blow up before my very eyes.

Nothing happened. My pneumatic air bottle had been burst wide open, my guns wouldn't work. Should I ram him? Could I bail out if I did? Sense and sensibility. Don't allow the adrenalin to control the brain. Become like an advowee, take pains to prepare to present a curate to the benefice in the Church of England.

I rolled her on her back, hauled on the stick and dived towards the heaven-sent blessing of the cloud layer, pulled her out at tree-top level and nursed the Spitfire back to Biggin Hill where further trauma was ready and waiting. If my air bottle was smashed, which it clearly was, then my brakes wouldn't work for they also relied on pneumatic pressure. Furthermore, my R/T was in little pieces, meaning that I could not ask for emergency treatment from the airfield controller, and for all I knew my Spitfire was disintegrating fast. My German is not good, but something like this occurred to me: *Die Nachwelt ist mir gleichgultig – Ich schreibe fur heute* – I don't care for posterity, I'm writing for today. I turned on the final approach for the longer runway, no flaps of course for they also relied on my (smashed) air bottle selected undercarriage down and nothing happened, for the undercarriage positioning also relied on compressed air. But there was an emergency air bottle for occasions such as these, so I hopefully pressed the tit – rather difficult to do with only one hand which also was in total control of the Spitfire – and to my astonishment, I saw the red lights extinguish and eventually the green lights appear. This locked my undercarriage down. (I was a fool; I should have belly-landed the aircraft and saved myself further travail.) As I was approaching the threshold of the main runway, I noted with anguish that two squadrons of Spitfires were lining up on the secondary runway, and the first section was moving forward purposefully to take off. The fact that they would collide with me just after my point of touchdown was hard luck. I was totally committed to landing, I was flying a one-armed bandit, and my wounds were hurting like hell.

I plonked the Spitfire down, ducked as a couple of Spitfires taking off missed my head by inches, relaxed as she rolled on down the runway with an inexorable inevitability. I applied the brake lever, a futile endeavour, and saw the curtains begin to close over my short-lived life. As the barbed wire at the end of the runway loomed up, and I was proceeding at 45 mph minimum, I flung the death-wish from my face, banged on the starboard rudder-bar, gave the Merlin a burst of throttle to assist the process of turning sharply to the right, hoped that the undercarriage would not collapse under the stresses, and she reacted according to my wishes as my Spitfire normally did. She wheeled me off the runway, ran along the grass, and friction caused her to slow down to about 30 mph, but she was pointing directly at my squadron dispersal hut, and I was now too weak to do anything about it. When they saw this tumbrel approaching them quite fast, the airmen, wisely, decided to run like hares in all directions. The only concession to gaiety is a striped shroud, they say. I wasn't feeling gay, nor was I somnambulistic. I have always been a fatalist, and anyone who aspires to be a fighter pilot and is not possessed of that quality has made a wrong decision. I just awaited events. I had put my final chip on the roulette table.

Events then took control. The wheels of the Spitfire banged into a filled in bomb crater, she reared onto her nose, thought for a moment she would break her neck and mine by turning onto her back, decided not to, and stuck on her nose. The ground crews removed themselves from behind their barricades, and hurried to the scene. They couldn't chisel the cockpit canopy open, for two bullets had struck the runners, and it was jammed tight shut as a Prime Minister's mouth at Question Time. However, they got hold of two enormous jemmies and a sledge-hammer, and beat the canopy off its mountings. Undoubtedly, the nearest I came to death was when they were removing me from the debris.

With all too much enthusiasm, six of them clambered onto the fuselage, undid my safety harness and parachute straps, and then began to manhandle me out of the cockpit. Part of me they began to drag away was my severely damaged arm, but a few shrieks of agony and some old-fashioned English brought their ebullience to an abrupt halt. As the blood-wagon drew up, with the fire engine in close attendance, more skilful hands removed me from the wreck, and I was driven to the sick bay. The medical wallah offered me some sweet tea, and I offered him a punch on the nose if he didn't give me a hefty glass of rum. I was then trundled to Guy's Hospital which had been dispersed to Orpington, where an Indian surgeon performed an immaculate operation under X-ray conditions and removed chunks of lead from my arm, amongst other patchwork.

Although the nurses attracted me very much, I decided that I was not also in love with the hospital. So two days later I demanded to see the boss of the hospital and told him I was discharging myself.

'You can't do that!' he exclaimed. 'Your wounds need hospital treatment for at least another month.'

'But you must realize,' I replied, 'that there's a war on. Every able-bodied pilot is urgently required in the front line.'

'But you are not able-bodied!' he shrieked.

'Of course I am,' I said. 'I landed the wreck with one hand, didn't I? So I can clearly take off a serviceable Spitfire with one hand.'

He had no reply to that and gave me my discharge, together with bundles of bandages, various medicaments and the rest.

My Spitfire had forty-three bullet-holes in it, plus a murderous gash from an explosive cannon shell.

7

On the Move with Athol

As previously related, Bobby Oxspring took command of B Flight in October 1940, an obvious selection. He joined No. 66 Squadron before the war, learned his craft on Gauntlet biplanes, and assisted to re-equip the squadron with Spitfires. He destroyed five German aircraft and shared in the destruction of three more during the Battle of Britain, went on to do a lot more damage to the Luftwaffe, and finished the war with a DFC and two bars, plus the Air Force Cross – for gallantry 'not in the face of the enemy'.

Bobby was a good pilot and a crack shot – I should know. He and I were on a sortie one day and we spotted four Me-109s. I covered his tail as he attacked one of them, and he blew the canopy of the German fighter off at extreme range, about 400 yards. I then lost him and disposed of another German fighter, but we both landed OK. Good shooting, Bobby! I was promoted to command A Flight a month or so later, so Bobby and I became the subordinate backbone of No. 66 Squadron. (The real strength, of course, was reliant on the squadron commander.) Eventually, Bobby became exhausted, because he worked harder in terms of operations than the human frame and mind are designed for. He most certainly did not ask to leave No. 66 Squadron because of this but, as I will record, fortune brought the process about – otherwise, as they say, he would have died in harness.

When I was given command of A Flight, as the senior of the two flight commanders Bobby would assume command of the squadron in the absence of the squadron commander. In such circumstances, I came under his command, but otherwise we worked in harness together, and we were good friends. I was at home on sick leave, trying to regain my memory after being severely concussed when I ran into the barbed wire surrounding the airfield at Hawkinge, in October, when Rupert Leigh was promoted from the job as Officer Commanding No. 66 Squadron. I was utterly shaken when on my return I learned that Rupert was no longer with us; we had been in the most intimate circumstances of all, for I was his permanent wing-man in action; we were most certainly comrades in arms, and our friendship has blossomed over the years. He had handled No. 66 Squadron with the greatest gallantry, but his outstanding attribute can be summed up in the word 'leadership', not necessarily of the conventional kind, most certainly not as an actor with the part of 'Martinet'. I summed it up quite neatly elsewhere, when I wrote that he kept our morale at high pitch, in the most difficult circumstances, and that required a magician's cunning. He did it mainly by being almost always in the lead of the squadron in the air, and by his wild, extraordinary sense of humour. I mark him as one of the great men I have known.

Athol Forbes was barely on the hot seat when I got back to the squadron, and he was about the only man I would have found acceptable to take the chair from Rupert. He had held the difficult assignment as flight commander in No. 303 (Polish) Squadron, and sported a DFC and bar, and the Polish VC, the Virtuti Militari. The Poles were experienced, often brilliant, fighter pilots, but they were wild enthusiasts, individualists, and preferred to go it alone, not under the British discipline of squadron formations – until they were broken up and one was on his own, as we almost invariably were. Added to this was the language difficulty, for some of the Poles hardly had any English over the R/T. The outstanding fighter pilot on the British side in 1940 was a member of No. 303 Squadron; he was a Czech, Sergeant-Pilot Frantisek, with seventeen confirmed victories. Another pilot among the top ten was Flying Officer Urbanowitz, also a member of No. 303 Squadron. According to the record, Athol had seven confirmed victories when he joined No. 66

Squadron. He spoke French fluently, a great asset when dealing with the Poles whose second language was often French. Like Rupert, Athol was about ten years older than myself. Like Rupert, he was a product of an English public school, Dover College, although he let it be known that he was born a Scot and proud of it.

Athol was God's gift to women, and I am not going to suggest that he did not enjoy that prerogative. He was a lean, tough, muscular six-footer, and always dressed with impeccable fastidiousness even under field conditions. His hair was immaculately trimmed, and his finger-nails well manicured. It is not unlikely that Ian Fleming modelled his James Bond on Athol, for he had all the attributes. In profile he looked like the devil incarnate, a swoop of a Roman nose, tight lips, hair curling from the fringes like horns, and a determined, set chin. Face on, he was quite different. Green eyes, crooked lips with slightly crooked teeth, amiable, pleasant of countenance, but with an obvious underlying strength in his facial bone structure. To top it, he was an expert in judo. At a drunken brawl in the officers' mess at Biggin Hill, an intoxicated senior officer, for some odd reason, decided to leap on to Athol's back and strangle him. Athol had, no doubt, imbibed, but he had the capacity to drink a camel under the table and remain strictly sober. I waited with awe when I saw the officer on the point of committing *felo de se*. Athol pretended not to notice that an eleven-stone drunk was crouched on his back attempting to garrotte him. He bided his time, suddenly used his feet like a ballet dancer, got the officer in a judo hold, and threw him fifteen feet across the room. As I watched the man flying like a space missile on take-off in mid-air, I thought about the Coroner's inquest. However, he merely struck his head with considerable force on the wall, lay unconscious for several minutes while we all went back to the bar, came to and rang up Sick Quarters. An ambulance duly arrived, the officer had himself X-rayed, found no bones broken – Athol knew too much about the Japanese art of *ju-jutsu* to break the silly little man's neck. (As a matter of fact, *ju-jutsu* or *jiu-jitsu* was a science of self-defence without weapons invented by the Chinese millennia ago. But the Japanese are great copyists.)

Apart from being a brilliant fighter pilot, Athol was also an expert car driver. The fact that he broke so many motor cars in head-on collisions during the period I served under his command detracts in no way from his expertise as a chauffeur. There are other explanations for this phenomenon. Athol was a connoisseur of food, wine and women; he was also a highly sophisticated man and I was just a kid. He knew all the hot-spots in London, whereas my knowledge was just confined to the Polytechnic Cinema in Upper Regent Street. But I had to learn fast or die in the attempt, and eventually I found I could take Athol to odd spots which even he knew nothing about. That, I think, was the finest achievement of my life.

When one considers I am discussing the period April 1940–February 1941, that involves only ten months. Yet, Bobby and I, together with very few other pilots, really were the hard core left of No. 66 Squadron from the time I joined it. Athol, after all, was a new boy – but mark it, he soon accepted and adopted the individual spirit of the squadron. Our ground crews were more or less intact, for our airfields were never bombed; we normally arrived at bombed-out airfields after the event.

Gravesend was certainly never bombed during the fifty-five days the squadron was based there; perhaps the Germans thought it was unworthy of their attention, being merely a pre-war airport. In fact, it was beautifully situated to do a great deal of harm to the Luftwaffe, and I think we succeeded. We could climb to the north on receipt of the scramble order, gain combat height and thereby get the jump on the Germans. We could cover London, no matter whether the bomber raids approached via the serpentine twists of the Thames from the east, or whether they attempted to burst their way through the thin blue line on an approach from the south-east. It is rather extraordinary, and shows the grave deficiencies in German air intelligence that Gravesend was never bombed. They made deep penetrations, for example, to Brize Norton in Oxfordshire, where training aircraft were based; indeed they destroyed forty planes. But their immediate task was to get rid of the front-line units in Fighter Command, and they certainly succeeded when they bombed Manston near Ramsgate, Hawkinge near Folkestone, Tangmere by Chichester, Biggin Hill – with its vital Operations Room – Kenley near Croydon, Hornchurch near the Thames Estuary, and the rest. Gravesend, however, although it contained only one fighter squadron, was of paramount importance; but fortunately for us, German intelligence had not taken it into account.

So, in the main, our ground crews had been members of the squadron for quite a long time, which was of incalculable benefit. Some of our senior NCOs had been posted elsewhere, some had even been given commissions as engineer officers. Our one-time corporals were now sergeants, our sergeants were flight-sergeants. But the strange, mystical, essential aura of squadron tradition and our high standards were all there. Newly joined ground crews, innocent as they might have been, were instilled with this mysticism almost on arrival. Newly joined pilots had to adopt our attitudes or suffer the consequences. (One who was too haughty, or proud, never conformed. He didn't suffer the consequences. We never acted in vitriolic fashion. I let him off the hook as I will not recount. I won't mention his name. *Folie de grandeur* is a kind of psychiatric condition. Poor chap, he suffered from that complaint. *Le nez de Cléopâtre; s'il eût été plus court* – one fears.)

The pace hardly slackened after 15 September; day after day, month after month, I watched the sun rise in its wrath. Athol was ordered to re-deploy No. 66 Squadron to West Malling, near Maidstone, on 30 October, which was extremely stupid of the staff at HQ FC. The airfield had recently been bombed, and there were no runways. Craters in the grass had been filled in with clay. Not surprisingly, we wrote off four Spitfires on landing, for their wheels buried themselves in the clay, and they reared on their noses, thus breaking the airscrews and making it necessary for the Merlins to be removed and be subjected to shock tests. We were billeted in a mansion near to the airfield, and the airmen had to survive under field conditions. We effected nothing worthwhile at Malling, but as bad weather had set in, we certainly got up to a lot of social nonsense. Merely a week later, Athol was ordered to move the squadron to Biggin Hill, where there was a Defiant squadron and two other Spitfire squadrons. Fighter squadrons do not like the company of others, and we were not at all impressed by our colleagues in the other squadrons. The Defiant was an anachronism, a two-seater 'fighter' with a rear gunner operating four machine-guns in a gun-turret which weighed a ton. Yet it had the same powered Merlin engine which drove the Spitfire and the Hurricane through the air, with all the implications thereby implied. It was not even aerobatic, and whoever heard of a non-aerobatic fighter? The death rate in the Battle of Britain among the Defiant squadrons was appalling, a matter of criminal negligence by the Air Staff who authorized the design specifications. But at this time it was being used in the role of night-fighter, and it was useless in that role.

A certain senior officer at Biggin ran a harem, where nude WAAFs languished sipping champagne, lying on satin sofas. Unfortunately, I was never invited to attend these séances. But the Air Officer Commanding, No. 11 Group, inadvertently paid a courtesy call one evening, and was either enthralled or appalled by the set-up. The senior officer referred to was given the Order of the Boot, but I have no idea what the AOC did about things afterwards.

Another squadron at Biggin was No. 92, and it was possessed of its own panache. The pilots were billeted in a mansion down the road, but they were vigorous, indeed enthusiastic. They had their jointly owned fleet of Cadillacs, their squadron dance-band comprised trained fitters and riggers and their mistresses. Night after night, the band would play and it was a first-class band; it even had a harpist. The food and wine was provided by a leading London caterer, and where the girls came from God known but I don't. The whole set-up equated with a gigantic brothel.

The other Spitfire squadron was under command of probably the finest fighter leader in history, Sailor Malan, a South African and one-time merchant seaman. He was tough, strict, a martinet and he and I could never have lived together. He destroyed about seven German aircraft during the Battle of Britain, and went on to kill more Germans than the average professional tramp has had hot dinners, when the fighter sweeps over France were instigated. But as a matter of fact No. 66 Squadron performed the first offensive fighter sweep in history under the command of Rupert Leigh. This was before the Dunkirk operation when we swept the area of the North Sea well beyond Smith's Knoll Lightship, because German naval activity was suspected. What we were supposed to do about the German Navy when we were armed with light 0.303-inch machine-guns, I haven't the faintest idea. But we saw nothing and returned to our forward base. Rupert, in due course, was sent a congratulatory signal for being the first man to lead a squadron of Spitfires on an offensive, as opposed to purely defensive, operation. I think he tore it up.

We spent most of our time at Biggin on soirées in London's West End. Athol conned from the Secretary of State for Air three large Ford shooting-brakes. The weather clamped down for several weeks, and due to our primitive instruments we could not take off – nor could the fighters of the Luftwaffe for that matter. So we would scream along in convoy to places like the Dorchester, the Grosvenor House, the ('We never closed') Windmill Theatre, the Regent Palace Hotel and so forth. London was under heavy bombing attacks at this time, but we merely ducked under tables, or preferably pulled young ladies onto the floor to give us a form of armour plate, and generally had a good time. Our convoy would return to Biggin Hill in the early hours, screeching along at 80 mph, turning and twisting to avoid loads of high-explosive and incendiary bombs en route. How we got away with it heaven knows, but I must confess it was rather terrifying at the time; in retrospect it was the most amusing moment in my life.

While based at Biggin Hill, my pilot's flying log-book has nothing much to record. When the weather cleared and interrupted our gorgeous social life, I do note that we were constantly engaging German fighter-bombers at great height. As related, we probably destroyed twenty Stukas over Dover on 14 December, and I almost certainly shot down four of those aircraft. I bailed out on 28 November when a half-witted sergeant-pilot collided with me at 15,000 feet. I was rescued by Mrs Dewar, her daughter and prospective son-in-law from the deadly clutches of the Home Guard, and they drove me to their house, Dutton Holmstead, near East Grinstead. She was the wife of a whisky distiller, and gave me some of her husband's product, which did me no harm at all. The house was later made into a hospital where badly burned and injured pilots were patched up, many of them now members of the Guinea-Pig Club – people like Richard Hillary, author of that fine book *The Last Enemy*. (The last enemy that shall be destroyed is death – and so it was when Hillary took off one dark night from a RAF base in Scotland. His fearful burns had barely healed. 'A golden bridge is for a flying enemy.')

Whereas Bobby Oxspring was Deputy Squadron Commander when Athol was away for a conference, or on leave, or whatever, it was not impossible that Bobby would also be away at the same time. Which left me fondling my favourite baby, No. 66 (Fighter) Squadron. And so it occurred on a number of occasions, more especially perhaps on 14 February 1941. Athol Forbes was taking a well deserved day off in London to do some shopping, and Bobby was in command. The controller, underground at Biggin

Hill, rang up and asked for a pilot to fly an RDF (radar) calibration sortie. The radar chain regularly required calibration flights, and these were fairly hazardous missions. Single aircraft were required to be flown half-way across the Channel at varying heights, when the radar operators would adjust their electronic equipment with accuracy, for the pilot detailed would report the height he was flying, his course, and so on. This left his R/T messages wide open to the German 'Y' Eavesdropping Service, and would put his life in dire danger if the Luftwaffe decided to scramble a flight of fighters to make an interception. I flew a number of such sorties, but we used only experienced pilots on these missions for obvious reasons.

And so came about the incident of 14 February of which I have already described the outcome. This was the background. Bobby informed the controller that he personally would fly the radar calibration mission. I suggested to him that I would fly the sortie, but Bobby pointed out that there were no plots on the operations table, and surely he might be left to fly on his own, leaving me in command of the squadron. There was not much wrong with his request, so off he went into the thin sky yonder. We sat around at fifteen minutes' readiness, playing poker and things as was our wont. Theoretically, controllers would only scramble us when we were at immediate readiness; in fact, they used to send us off when we were supposed to be at thirty minutes' readiness or even released.

On this occasion, the controller requested that I take the squadron off from a fifteen minutes' readiness posture immediately. I told him he was a series of four-letter words, but we were in the air fairly quickly, within about three minutes of the scramble order. That the controller was fairly useless was obvious to me since he should have raised our state of readiness when the hostiles first appeared over France on the radars. I also knew who he was, because I recognized the voice over the R/T, and I thought very little of his professional ability.

It was always a difficult problem with controllers *vis-à-vis* fighter leaders. The leader had to take the tactical decisions in the light of events as he saw them. However, a fighter leader could see for less than two miles at great height where the eyes have no frame of reference – and to scan into infinity may mean that the eyes are focused only a few hundred yards away, when looking at nothing. On the other hand, when looking at the stars and trying to identify them, the eyes are focused millions of light-years distant – there is a difference! Whereas when the leader is blind because a raid is out of his sight, the controller may not be blind, he might be 'seeing' a raid a hundred miles away. Perhaps more important was the fact that the leader had no idea – because of the ludicrous procedures utilized in 1940 – how many other squadrons were being directed onto the same raid. It is too technical to outline here, but I have explained it elsewhere.

The best controllers were pilots with recent operational experience who had been too severely wounded, or burned, to fly and reluctantly took their seat on the controller's dais. They had a tactical sense, they knew they were acting merely as intelligence agents to flying leaders, they wouldn't attempt to place him up-sun of the raid or to indulge themselves in aerial tactics in any way. They gave the leaders all the information at their disposal and left him to sort out the mess on his own.

In the main, however, controllers were 'wingless wonders', as officers in the RAF who did not spend their time flying were termed. This is not intended to be disparaging to controllers in general, because most of them realized the problems of squadron leaders and acted accordingly. They could never, of course, possess the instinct born of experience of the flyers, but they were sensible enough to appreciate this essential point. Some of the non-flyers did manage to obtain the power of instinct, but some of them thought they were kind of Napoleons directing a battle and that we were under their generalship. An egotist is a person of low taste, more interested in himself than me and

my squadron. Some controllers imagined that squadron
leaders were under their *orders*, which we never were. In
truth, they were our advisers, just part of our intelligence
sources.

However, when we took to the air on 14 February, I had
no inhibitions – apart from the fact I thought very little of the
controller's proficiency. I was well experienced in leading the
squadron into action. The majority of the pilots on the flight
were pretty raw, but two or three knew what they were up to.
On the ascent I reported cloud base at about 10,000 feet, and
I estimated it would be 3,000 feet thick with blue skies above.

'Maintain your vector of one eight zero degrees,' the
controller told me. 'Penetrate cloud. Ten miles to the south
will be approximately fifty bandits of the fighter type,
estimated altitude 25,000 feet.'

Penetrate cloud when Messerschmitts 109 in wing
formation would have a height advantage of 15,000 feet, ten
miles distant! Penetrate cloud, when we would be clearly
silhouetted against the cloud layer, when they would be up-
sun of us! I was talking to a lunatic. On the other hand, I
could hardly indulge in a *conversazione* with this fat-head
and write him a thesis on fighter tactics. Short R/T
communications were essential, else the German 'Y' Service
would have given the German wing leader information at the
drop of a hat as to our exact location, and further useful
tactical information.

'Seen your psychiatrist lately?' I inquired. 'What other
units do you have under control?'

'Position under control,' he replied sharply.

All my instincts throbbed. The obvious solution was to
level out below cloud, gain combat speed, wait for two
minutes, climb through the cloud as fast as possible,
continue on course until we had the height advantage over
the Messerschmitts, turn onto a reciprocal heading, and get
them on the jump as they turned for France and their French
girlfriends. Against that, I had been informed that the
position was strictly under control so, like a fool, I climbed

the squadron through the cloud, put the pilots into battle formation as we proceeded on the climb at too low a speed for combat, and suffered the consequences.

After repairs and minor modifications, I released myself from Guy's Hospital, as previously related, but found that I had my right arm firmly in a sling. It was to stay that way for a further month.

Very shortly afterwards, Athol Forbes was ordered to re-deploy the squadron to Exeter 'on rest'. Fighter Command HQ thought we had suffered enough travail. We probably had, but we didn't feel in need of a 'rest'.

8

Why the City of Exeter was Blitzed

Among the scores of RAF stations I have served at, there is not the slightest question but that my favourite, far and away, was Tangmere, which lies a few miles to the east of Chichester. I served at Tangmere on half a dozen occasions in peace and war, and had the honour to command the two famous fighter squadrons, Nos 1 and 43, which gave the station its backbone, and made it the crack fighter airfield in Fighter Command for a generation and more. (We are intending to open a museum at the now defunct fighter station, and it should be open to the public soon.)

Biggin Hill did not appeal to me; it lacked character despite the fame it acquired during the war. I remember it best for two reasons. It was there that I really learned how to handle a motor-car. I bought a marvellous Lagonda four-seater touring car, with a hood, a strap to hold the bonnet down at 100 mph, and all the trimmings. In the winter of 1940, when the snow lay on the runways, or they were covered with ice and it was impossible to get our Spitfires into the air, I used the main runway as a kind of racing track. When the thumping great engine was nice and warm, I had a smooth surface over a mile long to drive the car at maximum speed. It was also fun, and instructive, to gain speed to 60 mph and then jam the brakes on and try to keep the car straight as she skidded on the ice. It was even greater fun to deliberately put the Lagonda into a kind of horizontal spin, which was achieved by turning hard on the steering-wheel, simultaneously jamming on the brakes, and rotating fast. I once managed to keep her in a 'spin' for eight rotations, turning as fast as a whirligig. Again one would spin her and try to correct so that I was pointing in the direction I wanted to go. When I got the knack, it wasn't too difficult to straighten the car within seconds of putting it out of control. The police had nothing on me when I had conquered these arts. (I don't know how I would fare today, because I haven't made my escape from their clutches latterly.)

The other major recollection of RAF Biggin Hill revolves around the fact that I acquired a small cocker-spaniel bitch while I was there. I named her Pookie, which was a rude word in Malaya. One day, to my horror, I found her clutched in the sexual embrace of Sailor Malan's mongrel fox-terrier. I rushed her to a vet, who did what he could, but, alas, to no avail. She produced six strange-looking puppies in due course, and she produced them on my wool-lined leather flying coat, much to my chagrin. I and my batman fed the pups until they were of an age, whereupon I gave them away to decent homes. I suppose that this incident made me a kind of brother-in-law to Sailor Malan.

People recount all sorts of things relating to the extra-sensory perception of dogs, most of which I do not believe. What I do know to be true, however, is something rare and strange. Pookie always used to follow me to my Spitfire, sit and wait until I started the engine and taxied away. What I did not know for several months, until a number of pilots and ground crews informed me, was that she would chase my aircraft as I taxied to the end of the runway, when she would again sit on her haunches while I took off. Furthermore, she would stay on her haunches ignoring other aircraft landing and taking off, remaining immovable. *But*, when I came in to land, she would take to her feet and rush after my Spitfire, the whole length of the runway, along the perimeter track, following close behind my aircraft. What I did observe was that she was almost invariably sitting near my aircraft whenever I climbed out of the cockpit.

'If your own dog doesn't take to you and greet you with affection, you can make up your own mind that there's a yellow streak in you.' It's true, you know.

There were plenty of girls around at Biggin Hill, but I didn't get up to any fancy stuff. One in particular attached herself to me, and indeed visited me during my short stay at Guy's Hospital. Also, don't ask me how, but an 'army officer' attached himself to the squadron dressed in the uniform of a Captain RA. We gave him a room in the officers' mess at Biggin. He had also had a flat at Chatham when we were based at Gravesend. Uproarious parties were held there, and we would sleep on the floor of the flat until such time as we had to leave to be at readiness at first light. He seemed to be very rich and used to give us lavish presents – he gave me some silk pyjamas when I was in hospital. We never questioned his credentials. He obviously loved the glamour of being accepted by a fighter squadron as one of their own. It did occasionally cross my mind why he was not on duty with his regiment, but it appeared that he was on permanent sick-leave because his lungs were weak. In the course of time it dawned on me that he had homosexual tendencies, not that he ever tried anything on me for it must have been pretty obvious that I would have put my shoe in his eyeball if he had. Let us call the girl in question Peggy Brown, to preserve her anonymity, and the man Captain Bloggs. They will enter the sequence of events later.

We waited at Biggin Hill until our relief squadron arrived, and burst our ribs laughing when they crashed four Spitfires in an attempt to perform a split-arse landing to indicate to us how jolly good they were. Then Athol took No. 66 Squadron off and set course for Exeter Airport. My arm was still in a sling, but I found another pilot to drive me and Pookie and our luggage to Exeter. It was a difficult car to drive, was the Lagonda, and he drove it very badly, much to my chagrin.

Athol, of course, arrived long before I, and we found the airport much to our liking – except for the fact that it had been developed for operations by Coastal, not Fighter, Command. The taxi-tracks were far too long and tortuous for us to have a hope of a quick scramble. The Spitfire was a brute to taxi, because she sat back on her tail-wheel, and her nose reared high in the air, obliterating all forward vision when moving on the ground. But one always had to be careful to avoid obstructions which might be there on the perimeter track, such as petrol bowsers, airmen on bikes, workmen making repairs and so on. Thus one had to proceed crab-wise, swinging the nose on the brakes, in order to see obliquely ahead. But the runway was more than long enough for our purpose, the weather factor not too bad, and the squadron already in residence was comprised of pleasant people.

This was a Hurricane squadron, No. 504 City of Nottingham (Auxiliary) Squadron. In command was Tony Rook, and one of his flight commanders was his cousin Michael Rook. More often than not, the Auxiliaries were the sons of rich men, weekend flyers before the war. The Rooks were sons of rich men, I believe, both were tall and big with it, and they both sported enormous moustaches. They were charming men, and later they both went to Russia with No. 504 to give support to the suspicious Soviets shortly after the German invasion. Tony was given the Grand Cross of the Order of Lenin or something, which allowed him free travel on the Moscow Underground, and the use of any ballet dancer of his choosing, whether male or female, for sexual purposes. I doubt very much if Tony took advantage of any of these facilities. A few years later, when I was appointed to the Staff of HQ No. 12 (Fighter) Group, Tony was my boss. We spent most of our office hours playing bridge, and he was better at the game than I was. Michael, alas, was killed in the war, and what a splendid chap he had been. I kept in touch with Tony after the war, but it is now many years since I saw him.

Honiton was up the road from the airfield; there they make lace among other things. But our social target was the city of Exeter, an easy drive on a westerly heading. Apart from the hardships of food and clothes rationing, the population didn't know, so to speak, that there was a war on. They eyed my arm-in-the-sling with some curiosity, so did many of the officers stationed at the airfield. (The Rook cousins knew that there was a war on for they had both indulged in combat during the Battle of Britain.) However, one officer asked me a question, rather tentatively, one day.

'What happened to your arm?' he inquired. 'Were you hit by a bomb in the London Blitz?'

'No,' I replied. 'I was pissed out of my mind, and I fell down the stairs.'

We made full use of hotels such as the Rougement, where the proprietor's daughter was a pretty, charming girl. She was aged about eighteen, innocent as a virgin, which she undoubtedly was. I made no attempt to give her tuition, but she was nice to have around. The Clarence Hotel, with its famous historical background, was another of our haunts. We had to wear uniform all the time in those days, and there is no doubt that we wandered around clothed with an air of glamour. (The fact that three-quarters of our pilots had never fired their guns in anger had nothing to do with it.)

I was embarrassed when I received a letter from the aforementioned 'Peggy Brown'. She would be taking a train to Exeter, and would I arrange for a room in an hotel and meet her at the railway station. Bourgeois marriage has put our country into slippers, and will soon lead it to the gates of death. I had not the slightest intention of getting married at that time; she, clearly, was determined to fix things so I would become her everlasting husband. However, I duly met her at the railway station, drove her to the Rougement, and saw her into her room. For how many days would she be residing in Exeter, I inquired. For a week, she told me, sticking out her jaw. She was a most determined young woman. I pointed out I would be on flying duty during the days which she would spend at Exeter, and I might even be at readiness during the nights – not the kind of readiness which I conceived she was awaiting. She realized that, she explained. Duty has to be given priority over love. (I was by no means in love with her, although she was a nice girl to have around – but not around my neck.) It became clear to me that I would have to give her the brush-off, or be suffocated. So I did.

One evening, Peggy and I were sitting in the lounge of the Rougement, sipping drinks, talking about no music in particular. The daughter of the proprietor of the hotel turned up, I introduced her to Peggy, and she and I talked pleasantries while Peggy scowled. When the daughter of the proprietor left us, I stuck my hand up Peggy's skirt, felt her warm thigh and went no further. She blushed, and said with considerable acerbity: 'You have changed! You never used to do that to me before! You are obviously in love with *her*!' pointing in the vague direction of the daughter of the proprietor of the Rougement Hotel.

I bent my head as if in despair.

'Watch it,' I replied. 'Women who love the same man have a kind of bitter freemasonry. I don't want that girl you refer to to stick a knife in your gullet. That's what they do, you know, or rather make the threat, when you join the Freemasons.'

And praise be to all the saints, and the devils, and the scorpions, she demanded that I drive her to the station to catch an early-morning train next day. However, Peggy's sister, whom we will call Jane, was another kettle of fish. But my lips are sealed, my quill is blunt, about what happened to Jane.

Operationally, we mainly wasted our time and resources at Exeter. We were by now equipped with Spitfires Mk 11, rather more powerful than the Mk 1, and things like the cockpit heating system actually worked. But we still had our puny batteries of eight 0.303-inch machine-guns as our armament, whereas the Messerschmitts carried two 20-mm cannon and a couple of heavy machine-guns. We were back with the role of escorting coastal convoys in the main but we did perform the occasional sweep over France. At about this time, the Luftwaffe put into squadron service the formidable Focke-Wulf 190. British Intelligence was so pathetically poor that we had no knowledge of this versatile fighter. It was a highly manoeuvrable, radial-engine fighter, with heavy armament. Reports from pilots who had been engaged and escaped with their lives began to filter back to Air Intelligence, who, or so it seemed to me, thought that the pilots were suffering from hallucinations. Clearly, if their advanced intelligence sources knew nothing about it, then this German fighter could not possibly exist! To mollify the pilots who had managed to escape from the deadly clutches of the FW-190, Intelligence asked them to draw their impressions of the fighter on paper, and went on to perform a sort of Identikit operation, which was not of the slightest use. To us, as Churchill put it in another context, it was a riddle wrapped in a mystery inside an enigma. And we did not like fighting against entirely unknown odds.

However, the problem was resolved when a half-witted German pilot landed a FW-190 intact on what is now known as Swansea Airport on the Gower Peninsula. Swift action prevented him from taking off again, or destroying his aircraft when even he realized he had landed in Britain. (He thought he was landing somewhere on the Brest Peninsula!) Then our test-pilots were able to evaluate the FW-190 for what it was worth, and it was very good, especially in terms of manoeuvrability. The radial engine also made it less vulnerable than the glycol-cooled, in-line engines of the Spitfire and Messerschmitt. The Spitfire Mk V was in production at this stage, a hotted-up version of the Mk II with two 20-mm cannon and a total of four machine-guns in the wings. (The real solution was to give it an armament of four, even six, 0.5-inch Colts. This was a devastating weapons system, because the mighty 'Point-Five' was a fast-firing, minor cannon and would allow much more ammunition to be loaded in the gun bays than 20-mm shell. With the basic armament of six Point-Fives, American fighters cleared the skies over metropolitan Germany later in the war. The Flying Fortress bomber also carried a dozen or so Point-Fives, which gave them their formidable defensive fire-power. Bomber Command had to cope with 0.303-inch machine-guns in defence due to the myopia of the Air Staff. Yet the Point-Five would have been made available to the RAF in about 1933! The Browning machine-gun we used was an American Colt design of lighter calibre than the Point-Five, constructed under licence by the Birmingham Small Arms Company.)

But the conventional Spitfire Mk V was simply not good enough to face up to the FW-190. The wing-tips were removed to give it faster aileron control, and the supercharger in the Merlin was 'cropped', which allowed the pilot to use more boost than heretofore. Rolls-Royce had been aware that the engine would be perfectly safe, and equally reliable, if the amount of boost available had been increased. But again, the dead hand of the Air Staff would not allow this essential modification, and God knows how many fighter pilots were killed through this unimaginative approach. But the modified Spitfire Mk V still could not really cope with the FW-190, and modified marks of the Messerschmitts. It was not until the Spitfire Mk 1XB came on the scene that our fighters could match those of the Luftwaffe. It is a pathetic history, for the Spitfire, in essence, was the finest conventional fighter in the war, although the American Mustang was far more versatile because of its eventual extremely long range, and its more effective armament.

When I detailed myself to fly weather reconnaissance flights from Exeter, I would occasionally take a trip to the Channel Islands, to display RAF roundels, or show the flag, to the hapless Britons living there under the German jack-boot. One had to be a bit careful to avoid being shot down by flak – there was small hope of German fighters doing the job, for I flew so low across the sea that their radars could hardly have spotted me. Furthermore, I would whiz so low and fast over the islands that the flak gunners hardly had a chance of success. I would waggle my wings over the major towns of

Jersey, thus displaying RAF roundels in all positions, and continue to fly fast and low over other of the islands. Whether it bucked up the morale of our off-shore people or not, I don't know – I thought it might. Anyway, it was a welcome relief from escorting convoys proceeding at five knots.

At Exeter, Athol taught me one of the essential factors that turn a person from a man to a leader of men. I believe that there was always a mutual regard between myself and my engine-fitter and aircraft-rigger, also with the NCOs whose paths and mine crossed. Since I always preferred to harmonize my own machine-guns, for example, to form a cone of lethal bullets 250 yards ahead of my Spitfire, I would attend the gun-butts when my aircraft was due to have its guns harmonized. The job entailed jacking up the tail end of the Spitfire and, with the use of spirit-levels, ensuring that the aircraft was in a straight and level position as if in flight. Then I would climb onto the wing and place a kind of periscope into each machine-gun in turn, which showed exactly how the gun was pointing. The idea was to have each gun adjusted to aim at a small cone on a screen, 250 yards away in the gun-butts. The armourers would adjust the guns according to my requirement as I checked their alignment through the periscope. I would centre each gun on a spot, but when firing in the air, the vibrations to the Brownings as they shot out bullets at a very high rate would create a cone of fire intense within a circle of about ten feet, but also with a spread in the form of a cone reaching for about sixty feet wide by forty feet high. If one fired at a range of less than 250 yards, so much the better in terms of destroying a German aircraft – because sighting errors are lessened with close-range shooting. If I opened fire at 400 yards, the bullets would cone in when I was at 250 yards, and would centre out to create an even wider – i.e. less lethal – cone of fire. But normally, on a good attack one would be closing range rapidly, and it would not take long to range to 250 yards, breaking off the attack at about 100 yards. If this sounds complicated, then it was!

However, in the terms described above, my 'leadership' was of a kind of individual nature. But Athol taught me how to deal with a whole squadron of pilots and aircrew, not just a small team.

'Tell all the chaps to assemble outside the squadron offices in half an hour's time – except for those on essential duties,' he instructed me one day. 'I'm going to give them a pep-talk.'

'OK, Sir,' I replied. 'You don't want them in formal parade order, I hope?'

'No. None of that bullshit. I just want to give them an informal pep-talk.'

We brought them to attention when Athol duly arrived, but he was carrying with him a soap-box of sorts, which the Officer i/c Trooping the Colour on the Horseguards never does. He stood the assembled officers and airmen easy, climbed onto his soap-box and gave them an oration they never forgot. He was as good at public speaking as at most things, was Athol. In essence, he told them that the normal professional, military custom was to punish people who disobeyed, or whatever, and apart from handing out a few gongs for valour, or devoted service, silence descended when a unit got along with their work in a satisfactory manner. He wanted them to know that the general behaviour and high standards shown by the officers and men under his command for the last several months was greatly to be commended. He was proud of every man-jack on the squadron, and he thought it high time he said so. He did not want our high standards to flag, but he saw no harm in publicly announcing that he appreciated, and was grateful for, the total effort of personnel in No. 66 Squadron. Finally, he said that he would pay for all the drinks for a period of one hour in the sergeants' and airmen's messes that evening. (Which must have cost him a fortune!)

He then dismissed the 'parade' and we went our various ways.

'Got the point?' he inquired as we wandered back to his office.

I nodded. 'Yes. I've got the point,' I replied.

I have never forgotten the point – show appreciation when appreciation is due. That's what is wrong with British management today.

I was at immediate readiness one evening when the controller rang me on the hot line and said he had radar plots of a force of German bombers approaching Exeter. Would I take off with my number two and patrol the airfield at 2,000 feet?

'Sure,' I replied. 'But why don't you scramble the whole of my flight? The rest of my pilots are at fifteen minutes' available. I could get them airborne very shortly after I take off.'

'Don't worry old boy,' he replied. 'The situation is under control.'

Dusk was falling, but the higher you climb, the more you demote nightfall. At 30,000 feet, night does not fall for well over half an hour compared with conditions on the ground, for example. Equally, by climbing at first light, one sees the dawn break a good half an hour before mortals living on earth ever do. However, at only 2,000 feet, there was not much difference between the earthbound and the fliers. So dusk continued to fall until I could barely discern the outline of the airfield directly below me. At about which moment, the controller rang me over the R/T and informed me that six Heinkel 111s had been identified crossing the coast en route to Exeter. And he went on: 'I have Hurricanes in pursuit. Land immediately.'

'A bloody Hurricane couldn't catch a Heinkel,' I replied. 'Please scramble my flight.'

'I order you to land, Red Leader. Else you will confuse the situation.'

'Message received and understood,' I replied formally. (Later in the war, we copied the Americans and

acknowledged by saying 'Roger'. Much more to the point.
Much less a waste of R/T time.)

I told my number two to go in and land, and hung around
covering the airfield until I thought the controller might
have a fit. Then I most reluctantly turned on the final
approach and landed in the dark – although I could still see
reasonably well at 2,000 feet. As I let the Spitfire roll to the
end of the runway, I heard great thumps and bangs. Then I
saw tracer bullets passing close to my head. I jumped out of
the Spitfire, ran like a rabbit with my parachute still strapped
on, banging on my legs, and jumped into a ditch. The
Heinkels were dropping sticks of bombs all over the airfield,
and the German gunners were firing merry hell at everything
around the place, including me. I removed my parachute,
and ran like a hare to the squadron dispersal, where we had
deployed a machine-gun on the top of the sandbagged
emplacement. One of our airmen, who was an engine
mechanic by trade, was blasting away with the machine-gun.
I reckoned I was a better shot than he was, so I took over the
gun from him, and fired a burst at the last of the Heinkels
overflying the airfield. There was little chance of hitting it,
for it was by then out of range. The bombers vanished into
the night almost as swiftly as they had arrived.

It was impossible to evaluate the damage done until dawn
the next day, but there was fair havoc. Several buildings were
destroyed, although I don't believe that the runway was hit.
There were craters all over the place and, worse even, lumps
in the ground indicating the presence below of unexploded
bombs. Red flags were soon stuck in to give further
indication of the presence of unexploded bombs, and it is
none too happy an experience to taxi your aircraft with its
wing over a lump in the ground, plus a red flag indicating the
presence of an unexploded bomb which might go off at any
time. Quite a bit of our servicing facilities was destroyed, and
our aircraft serviceability declined accordingly.

I did not discuss the matter with Athol Forbes. I believe
that with a little intelligence, and a smart piece of

controlling, I alone could have intercepted the raid before it arrived at the airfield. I would have seen the bandits all right, but the gunners would not necessarily have seen me. To me they would have been sitting ducks, and if I hadn't shot down three Heinkels, I would have cursed myself as useless. This would have broken up the raid before it was on target.

I think that this raid was a probing attack to test the defences around the city of Exeter. They found the defences to be negligible – whereas they were anything but, in fact. Therefore, with the inexorable logic of the Teutonic mind, the Luftwaffe decided that Exeter was an easy target for a night raid. Accordingly, in due course, they made a blistering attack on that gracious city and wrote off forever some of its monuments. It was my fault in a way – I ought to have ignored the instructions.

9

To Cornwall in Disgrace

After the bombing of Exeter airfield we were, not surprisingly, fairly disorganized. Permanent telephone communications had been cut, for example, and we had to rely on landlines laid down in haste and field telephones. Furthermore, the squadron officers had to move out of the officers' mess and take up accommodation in a requisitioned country house some miles from the airfield. There was insufficient squadron transport available to support such a re-deployment of resources, just to rub salt in the wound.

However, a day or two after the bombing, Bobby Oxspring's B Flight was supposed to be at fifteen minutes' readiness, which really meant that his pilots should have been in their shed at the airfield, but they were in our requisitioned billet. My A Flight was at thirty minutes' readiness, and we were in the house and could easily have come to immediate readiness, given the order, within the specified thirty minutes' time-interval. But we simply were not in telephone contact when the Group Controller contacted the operations desk in the pilots' hut and ordered Bobby's flight to take off immediately and land at an airfield in Cornwall for some unknown and probably spurious reason. Without going into too much detail, the Group Controller informed the Air Officer Commanding No. 10 Group, under whose aegis we now came, that No. 66 Squadron had failed to comply with his orders.

Quintin Brand was AOC No. 10 Group, a pilot with a distinguished record in the First World War, but he never piloted a monoplane to my knowledge, so could have had little understanding of the monoplane era. He was also renowned for being a martinet. What! This squadron from No. 11 Group not being able to attain the high standards of

10 Group! he no doubt conjured from his mind. Dammit! I'll teach them a lesson!

So he summoned an immediate Court of Inquiry into this piffling incident, thereby using up the valuable time of Athol, Bobby and myself; also the members of the Court, the witnesses, the shorthand writers and heaven knows who.

We three criminals, major perpetrators, had to stand in front of our fellow Lords and appeal in all humility in the terms that we were innocent. The Court tried hard not to giggle but with small success. Athol and Bobby explained the circumstances, but when it came to my turn I was fed up.

'I am entirely guilty of the charges,' I announced, and Athol nudged me in the ribs; clearly I was confusing his evidence. 'Furthermore,' I went on, 'I am responsible entirely for the whole cock-up.' That really confused the Court, because I clearly was not entirely responsible. But my intention, on the other hand, *was* to confuse the Court.

We were 'remanded' and went on as per norm, flying our aircraft. Eventually I was given a formal rebuke, and I forgot what happened to Athol and Bobby. What a waste of time and money!

Brand now had his eye on No. 66 Squadron. Shortly afterwards, Athol received instructions to re-deploy his squadron from Exeter to Perranporth in Cornwall. We didn't care at all; Cornwall would be as boring operationally as Exeter. In fact, if Brand had used his head, he would have re-deployed us to his easternmost airfield in Hampshire where we would have done a bit of good against the Luftwaffe over French airspace. But so it came to pass. Athol wearily wrote out yet another movement order, we packed our bags, and arrived at Perranporth airfield; we were the first squadron to operate from this strip of concrete. It wasn't newly opened; it wasn't even finished!

However, we left our 'Captain' Bloggs behind, because he had formed an attachment with No. 504 Squadron. We were glad to be shot of him. He was eventually hauled up before the High Court in Exeter, accused of wearing His Majesty's uniform under false pretences, being neither a member of the British Army, nor a commissioned officer. He was also accused of fraud on various counts, and finished up in Exeter gaol for a few years.

There were a number of disadvantages to Perranporth. The runway was sited a few hundred yards from steep cliffs and, a couple of hundred feet below, great rollers more often than not battered away at the cliffs. Hurricane-force winds were not uncommon, and gales were frequent. This brought two problems. Spume from the roaring sea covered our Spitfires with salt, also our motor-cars, and brought with it a slow erosion of both types of vehicle. We had to tie the Spitfires down, using large corkscrew pieces of metal to drive into the ground, and rope hawsers would be attached to both the wings and also the tail of the aircraft. Since we had only a single runway, it was not feasible to take off or land if high winds blew across the runway. We could cope with strong winds if they blew along the line of the runway with a maximum deflection of about fifteen degrees either way, but the Spitfire was prone to topple onto its nose when taxi-ing if strong winds were blowing. Our only recourse, therefore, was to arrange for two airmen to sit each side of the tail-fin to weight down the rear and check the tendency of the aircraft to be blown onto its nose which would have broken the propeller. It was all too easy to forget that one was taxi-ing with two 'passengers' and, indeed, I once arrived at a speed of 20 mph on take-off, happened to glance in my rear-view mirror, and saw to my great astonishment two airmen hanging on for grim death to my rudder fin. They were not merely getting the benefit of wind through the air at 20 mph from the gathering speed of the Spitfire, but also the total force of the slip-stream exuded by a propeller driven by an engine of 1,300 h.p. at full take-off boost. I hastily slammed on my brakes, came to a grinding halt and they climbed onto my wing. Their faces were not white with terror, they were green.

'Just thought I'd put the wind up you, chaps,' I said casually.

'Well, you didn't succeed,' one of them replied. 'We knew you were playing silly buggers and we wouldn't get airborne.'

I wasn't playing silly buggers! I had completely forgotten about them. Another few hundred yards on take-off and they would have indeed been airborne.

We had no hangars, of course, so aircraft had to be serviced often in storm conditions in winter weather. Athol had a reasonable office, and Bobby and myself had cubbyholes for our offices, as did our senior NCOs. There was some sort of canteen for officers, and another for other ranks, but our pilots' rest-room consisted of a large marquee situated close to the edge of the towering cliffs. Of course it blew down, as I will relate. And the old tin-mines of Cornwall, or some of them, were beneath the runway and the perimeter tracks. Someone normally drove round the tracks and the runway at dawn, just to see if anything unusual had occurred overnight. I was performing this chore early one morning, when I saw a hole in the perimeter track. I had a look at it; it was just about wide enough to drop a man through the hole. I found a large stone and dropped it down the hole, listening for echoes. There were no echoes. The pit was bottomless, and was obviously a shaft to an old tin-mine which had caved in. If a Spitfire's oleo-leg had gone into that hole, it would have written off a serviceable aircraft – today's value over £1m. The food in our 'mess' was awful, so Athol appointed our engineer officer – we had such breeds by now – as catering officer, and he swiftly improved things no end. Athol was also Camp Commandant, Officer Commanding both RAF Perranporth and No. 66 Squadron.

I was amazed at his organizational efficiency, which is not to say that commanding a fighter squadron does not require such effectiveness. But that aspect is one thing, whereas the seemingly trivial, in fact important, aspects of commanding a fighter base demand a differing kind of expertise. He was meticulous, always carried a notebook with him, and wrote down jottings when he saw that certain reforms were essential. Furthermore, he went to great lengths to ensure that the bureaucrats, and the RAF officers senior to him, achieved what he wanted. He was polite, coldly so when the occasion demanded, but he pushed hard when he saw the need for essential improvements. We didn't mind field conditions, but there does come a limit – we could hardly have operated using igloos. (My own approach was nothing like as subtle, or effective. I would let my hair down, use bad language, insult senior officers, curse bureaucrats, put people's backs up, until I got my way. Athol's strong but quiet diplomacy was, needless to say, on a much higher level then my own.)

We did not have an aircraft control tower or anything so sophisticated; nor was there a radio frequency via which we could talk to anyone who might be of help on the ground. If we were in trouble on the airfield circuit, we would beat up the pilots' marquee, nearly blowing it over as we did so, and waggle our wings. With luck another Spitfire would scramble, ask over the R/T what the trouble might be, close in in formation if necessary, and the pilot would visually inspect the offending aircraft.

On one occasion I selected undercarriage down, and the port oleo-leg stuck in the 'up' position, indicated by the fact that the starboard undercarriage warning light glowed green, whereas the other showed red. I climbed, increased the airspeed as much as I could, remembering that part of my undercarriage was down and it would have been torn off if I really pushed the throttle wide open, and thought. I put as much positive gee on the Spitfire as I could, waggled her round forcibly, in an attempt to make the recalcitrant oleo-leg unlock itself. Nothing happened, the ominous red light remained on. There were a few alternatives open to me, such as diverting to another airfield where there actually was R/T communication between air and ground, where the fire-engines and the ambulance would be ready and waiting to collect the pieces. But I much preferred to put the hulk onto the ground at my home station. Thus there was just one solution left, to plonk her down on one wheel and hope. I adjusted the controls so that she would land on her starboard wheel, came in quite fast to maintain aileron control for as long as possible, and when the wheel was happy with the runway, I put on full right aileron, simultaneously giving short blasts on the throttle to maintain her in a one-wing-down attitude.

I kept her in this configuration until the end of the runway became too close for comfort, then I let her do what she preferred. The Spitfire sank, with the gentleness of a person who had been deliberately prepared for consummation, onto her port wing. There were no sparks as the wings rubbed on the runway, and the airscrew didn't so much as clash with the concrete. As a matter of fact, all our fitters had to do with her was to jack her up, bash the offending oleo-leg down, haul her to the dispersal behind a tractor, and fix the locking mechanism. I was rather pleased about that; I never liked breaking Spitfires unnecessarily.

Our sector station was at Portreath, a few miles to the south. It contained an operations room, and the airfield was much larger than Perranporth which was its satellite airfield. At one time during our sojourn in Cornwall, a Czech fighter squadron was based at Portreath, and what a carefree bunch of pilots they were, considering they had nothing to lose but their lives. A number of them had their own violins, and would play soulful, wailing Bohemian music at the drop of a hat. They were comprised mainly of aristos, and they were devils with the women, which could have put our noses out of joint if we had flagged or failed in our personal endeavours in those Elysian fields from whence we gathered our beautiful, or not so beautiful, pieces of skirt.

A further advantage was that Jack Boret was our sector commander, a fine old war-horse, sage, just, encouraging, and full of sparkle. The three members of the hierarchy of No. 66 Squadron, Athol Forbes, Bobby Oxspring and

myself, had arrived under a cloud, brought about by the
Exeter affair. Jack Boret soon made it clear to me, anyway,
that he didn't give a damn about what a nonsense we were
purported to have made of things at Exeter; so far as he was
concerned, he said, he had mentally torn up the history
book, and he would assess us on our merit as we displayed it
to him. Not one of us three gave tuppence about what Brand
had decided in his wisdom, or lack of it, but it was helpful to
hear from our new immediate boss that he remained strictly
neutral over the affair.

On the advantageous side, the officers were given rooms at
the Droskyn Castle Hotel overlooking the great beach at
Perranporth. The whole of the top floor had been
requisitioned for officers' sleeping quarters by the Air
Ministry, and we were given beds, breakfast – at unholy
hours – and supper there. It was most comfortable, a two-
possibly three-star hotel. Holidaymakers still stayed at the
hotel, staid old couples taking a rest from the shambles of
living in London; but best of all, young female secretaries,
either with a friend or daring enough to make the journey on
the Cornish Riviera Express on their own. The guests
occupied the two main floors, and we were stuffed into the
(comfortable) attics. As our reputation spread, more and
more young women would arrive at the hotel, insisting that
they had rooms on the floor just below ours; i.e. within easy
range of our bedrooms. You might or might not despise sex,
but you can easily live with it. We lived with it, and the girls
had the finest holiday of their lives when they stayed within
touching distance of us. So that was certainly a benefit worth
recording.

Another advantage happened when the early summer
decided to glow, and those of us who were not at standby
used to drive down to the beach, dive into the sea, and get
beaten up by the breakers as they rolled majestically onward.
Cold water, maybe, but quite exhilarating. The undertow
was positively dangerous, so one had to beware. Apart from
his many attributes, Athol had a keen business mind. At the

far end of the beach, which was about two miles in length, someone spotted from the air a large lifeboat, washed onshore by the great waves. On receipt of this sighting, Athol had one of his good – but totally impracticable – ideas. He worked out the minimum number of pilots who should be at the airfield for operational purposes; by now, we had thirty or more pilots, which allowed for more than sufficient cannon fodder. The rest of us were to parade, with bathing trunks under our clothing, and proceed in a lorry under Athol's leadership, and salvage the lifeboat. We had hawsers and heavens knows what in the lorry. When the incoming tide lapped the boat, which was made of steel and weighed a ton or more, we shoved it into the sea having first attached hawsers to it. When it floated, we slowly and laboriously dragged it along to the little port of Perranporth. It was a long haul, and some of us were almost drowned when a bigger than usual wave swamped the boat and the haulers.

It was a long, tedious and hazardous operation, but somehow or other we floated it a couple of miles, got in position with our hawsers, waited for the right wave to roll in, and with a concerted effort beached the lifeboat by the port. Then we lay down, exhausted, on the beach.

'That, sir,' I said to Athol, 'was a hell of a good idea. But what are we going to do with the bloody lifeboat now?'

He gazed at me as if I was daft.

'It's perfectly obvious,' he replied. 'I'm going to buy a couple of Ford V-8 engines, get the fitters to service them, and fit them to the boat. Then we'll go trawling in it, catch enough fish, buy some potatoes on the cheap, and set up a fish and chip bar for the tourists. We'll make a fortune.'

'What a good idea,' I lied. 'But don't we need a propeller-shaft, a screw, a bit of instrumentation, a launching slipway, perhaps a sail or two, and little things like that? And how about some trawling nets? And how the hell are we going to set up a fish and chip bar? And who's going to cook the fish and bloody chips?'

Athol gazed at me, disappointment in his eyes.

'The trouble with you, old boy,' he said, 'is that you are always looking for the difficulties, the snags. You must show enthusiasm, enterprise and things like that. We've got our workshops, our fitters, we've even got a trained blacksmith. For that matter, we've got a serviceable enough Merlin engine from a wrecked Spitfire.'

He brooded.

'I don't see why we shouldn't put the Merlin in the lifeboat. I reckon we could get her up to twenty knots if we did.'

I was on the point of throwing my hands in the air in desperation, when a man in nautical uniform arrived on the scene.

'Who is responsible for this offence?' he inquired in a Cornish accent so broad it was almost incomprehensible.

'Oi bee,' Athol replied.

'In which case, zir, I 'ereby point out to you that I am 'is Majesty's Inspector of Wracks.'

'Surely you must mean wrecks?' I suggested.

'Oi zaid wracks, and Oi means bloody wracks. Oi've been awatching you through moi spyglass for the past four hours. You 'ave been interfering with 'is Majesty's property. Wracks washed up on this coast, and we get bleeding 'undreds in one year, belong to 'is Majesty. I am 'is Superintendent. I could put you lot in clink.'

'That's a lot of hog-wash,' I said. 'We've dragged the bloody boat from the end of the beach to the harbour. We've done you a favour. That's all we had in mind, to do you a favour.'

He took off his nautical cap and scratched his grey grizzled hair.

'I s'pose you 'ave indeed done me a favour, gentlemen,' he said. 'And thank ee for the favour.'

Us pilots wandered along to the lorry, somewhat disconsolately.

'It wouldn't have worked, sir,' I said to Athol.

'You're just a bloody pessimist,' he growled. 'Course it

would have worked. We would have made a fortune out of fish and chips.'

The next day a great roller bashed its way onto the beach by the harbour. It tore the lifeboat from the kind of anchorage the Inspector of Wracks had extemporized, and swept it out to sea. I was airborne and saw the hulk floating upside down. It was obviously a hazard to shipping, added to which my machine-guns needed exercise. I attacked it on three swoops, and armour-piercing bullets were included in my ammunition load. I watched it sink to the bottom. In which manner No. 66 Squadron did the Inspector of Wracks yet another favour.

My advice is never to make a blind date if you can avoid it, which is based on experience. We were constantly in telephonic communication with the Sector Operations Room at Portreath for all sorts of reasons. Part of our operational role, for example, was the protection of coastal convoys. We had our own Intelligence officer, with the name of Beaufort-Palmer, a man of extremely high intellect, obviously a product of Oxbridge, a gentleman in the best sense of the word, old by our standards – well into his thirties, I guess, a kind, wise person who, in the course of time, was to become my mentor and confidant. (I wish to God he had been our IO during the Battle of Britain; he might have made sense of our claims for enemy aircraft destroyed, instead of making nonsense as his somewhat brash predecessor succeeded in achieving.)

'Beau', as we called him, liked to keep a plot on the movement of convoys for our benefit, and he used to get his information from the Naval Liaison Officers in the Ops Room. When Bobby's flight was stood down, to allow the pilots and ground crew to go to lunch or whatever, and my flight relieved his, I would telephone the Ops Room to find out what the Met. officers thought about the weather prospects and so on. Not that I ever believed in their forecasts, nor do I to this day. As far as I was concerned, only

God and I knew how the weather would turn, and I proved it on countless occasions.

Convoy patrols were boring affairs, but we maintained constant surveillance over the ships; one section of Spitfires would not leave its patrol – except in emergency conditions brought about by a sudden decline in the weather – until the relieving section commander informed his colleague that he was in position. The most deadly boring patrol of them all was when the authorities decided to haul a floating dry-dock from Avonmouth to Portsmouth. It was towed by three ocean-going tugs, and escorted by a virtual flotilla of destroyers. It could only proceed at two knots, and it slowly made its way through our sector taking almost a week before it entered another fighter sector on an easterly course. If my Spitfire had been equipped with bombs, I would have sunk the bloody thing, because it gave me acute ennui.

However, when I talked to the Sector Operations Room, I became involved in conversation with one of its staff. She was in the WAAF, and she had a lovely voice. Either she would pass me on to someone more appropriate to the discussion, or she and I would indulge in conversation, sorting out the problem together. In my mind, I conjured up a vision of her. She was tall, a brunette, slim but with a good cleavage, her lips were lascivious, she was cultured, she wore no cuisses on her elegant thighs, her ankles were slim as a newly sprouting branch of a catalpa tree, her eyes were radiant purple – with a touch of wicked green – she was clearly the most aesthetically beautiful thing in the world. She would know all the arts of making throaty music, while palpitating sexually. There would be no need for a boudoir when I violated her with masculine intrusion; we would do the job on the very tip of Land's End, listening to the great waves roaring shorewards while we panted from our first huge enjoyment and settled down to have another go. In between times, I would gaze at her beautiful nakedness, massaging her in case she grew purple from the cold spume whipped up from the Atlantic, gazing at her glorious nudity

as Saint Theresa might have gazed at me, if I had uplifted her
skirt.

The whole thing was a piece of cake. So I made a date.

'When do you next have a day off, Corporal?' I inquired.

'Tomorrow, sir,' she replied demurely.

'Feel like a lobster lunch?' I suggested.

'But that would be marvellous,' she said, deepening her
lovely voice – she sounded rather better than Tallulah
Bankhead at her very best.

'OK, Corporal. I'll pick you up by the Dragon in
Portreath at mid-day. Wear a rose in your lapel so I can
recognize you. I'll be driving a large green Lagonda, so you
should recognize me easily.'

'But, sir,' she replied. 'I've got a photograph of you pinned
to the wall in my bedroom. I would recognize you
anywhere.'

Santa Maria! This would be the easiest job I ever pulled
off!

I rubbed my hands with glee and dreamt of my lovely lady
overnight, felt the cold Atlantic rushing over our bodies tight-
ly embraced, and the sheer joy of warming up this beauty in a
brow of Egypt, in a fine frenzy rolling. Why, with luck, I might
have to give her artificial respiration! Oh my God! Sleep came
scarce to me that night.

10

Operations

The next morning I told Athol I was taking a day off, leaving my deputy in charge of my flight. In theory, we were, under contract with the Air Ministry so to speak, allowed sixty-three days' leave every calendar year, although leave, whether for officers or airmen, was a privilege, not an entitlement. I am sure that the TUC would not approve of such a subtle clause in a contract between employer and employee; nor would they allow their workers to be on duty for twenty-four hours a day. In their reasoning they would be wildly out of touch, for our employer was His Majesty the King, not the Government – the Air Ministry simply acted the part as his agent. Secondly, we did not have in our midst a hard core of communist agitators! In any case, as the only leave I had taken for the past year or so was sick-leave, of course my squadron commander would not object to my taking a day off – he might have had it in mind to more or less order me to take a month off duty; I certainly had it in mind that he should do that on his own account.

So I put the Lagonda into first gear and rolled off in the direction of Portreath, my heart filled with the glow of the prospect, and in the pocket of my RAF tunic was a packet of contraceptives. I circumnavigated the one-track roads of that part of Cornwall, mounted a one-in-three gradient, only to come across another one-in-three on the immediate descent. The long Lagonda simply balanced itself on the top of the tip, and I heard grinding noises as the bottom of the engine struck terra firma, but the momentum of the Lagonda carried her forward and down we went, like you do at a Billy Butlin fairground. I glanced anxiously at the instruments and noticed a drop in the oil-pressure gauge, but the pump was still pushing oil into the cylinder block. I stopped at the first garage and took note of oil dripping ominously from the sump of the car, and asked the attendant to fill the sump to the brim with oil.

'Yee'll oil oop yeere ploogs,' he said.

'Oi be aware of zat,' I informed him.

I nursed the car to Portreath, arrived at the Dragon, and noted with horror a WAAF Corporal standing by the kerb. She was so young and so untender, and by comparison I had such a daily beauty in my life that she was ugly. I had really made a cock-up of my blind date, and despair overwhelmed me. My immediate impulse was to put my foot hard down on the Lagonda's accelerator, fly like the wind away from this object. Then commonsense, even compassion, took command. She was wearing a flower in her lapel. It was obvious to her that I was me – no one could fail to recognize the big, green Lagonda. To ignore her would be unthinkable, so I drew up to the kerb, opened the little passenger door of the car and invited her to hop in, which she did.

'I've got a problem,' I said.

'And what might that be, sir?' she inquired; her voice was as dulcet and lovely as it was over the telephone.

'I've cracked the oil-pump in the car,' I explained. 'I had intended to take you to St Ives and give you a lobster lunch. I also had it in mind to drive you to Land's End, just to watch the waves hurling themselves at the land. Music, sheer music, just like Fingal's Cave and all that, don'tcherknow.'

'How lovely that would be,' she sighed, sounding more like Greta Garbo than Tallulah Bankhead.

'In the circumstances,' I said mournfully, 'the best I can offer you is to take you to the nearest village away from here and give you fish and chips.'

'But I love fish and chips!' she mouthed.

I gave her fish and chips, drove her back to RAF Portreath, dumped her, staggered to a garage, filled up with oil, and nursed the Lagonda back to Perranporth. Then I put my fitters on to the cracked oil sump of the car. They patched it up in half an hour.

The motto of No. 66 (Fighter) Squadron is *Cavete Praemonui* – 'Beware, we strike'. Its crest is a rattlesnake poised to strike. I felt rather like a rattlesnake after that interlude, but I did happen to have my Lagonda go unserviceable on me – quite inadvertently. So I wasn't a complete cad, although I felt rather caddish, even taking all the circumstances into account.

The squadron complied with its motto and struck about a year after I joined the squadron – although we had spent quite a lot of our time striking during that year. We had a newly joined sergeant pilot, Bob Large, and I was educating him in the arts of fighter action. He and I were at immediate readiness one day when the controller rang up and ordered my section of two aircraft to scramble. He was enthusiastic and, as it turned out, also euphemistic. Radar reports, he told me, indicated a large blip about fifty miles south of the Eddystone lighthouse. He appreciated that the blip might signify perhaps a dozen German aircraft patrolling in that area. There was little time for conversation, but I told him to scramble a further two sections as soon as possible (ASP) after our departure. (He did no such thing, poor blighted fool.) Bob was a good pilot, but totally lacking in combat experience, which was why I was attempting to educate him. We got into the air soonest, and I set course for Eddystone. On arrival, I noted the great swell of the Atlantic battering fruitlessly at the concrete foundations of that enormous monument to British civil engineering.

'Maintain course, heading 180 degrees,' the controller informed me over the R/T. 'We are now getting a blurred picture from the radars, so use your own initiative. The bandits are at approximately 10,000 feet, heading on a westerly course. They are about twenty miles ahead of you. Your R/T signals are fading. I doubt if I can be of further assistance. Good luck.'

'Thanks,' I replied, 'But have you scrambled two more sections?'

There was no reply. Clearly I was now outside radio-telephone range of the controller; added to which, the icy cold Atlantic was showing its ferocity below, with white waves capping, and an enormous swell raging. This was no place for a couple of single-engine Spitfires. If one bank of sparking plugs had cut out for any reason, it would add up to ditching in those fearful seas. If one managed to scramble out of the cockpit after ditching, if the Mae West happened to work, Bob or I would be dead from exposure within a couple of minutes, granted those provisos. If the bandits we were chasing happened to get even one lucky shot which bust our glycol coolant systems, then we both, perhaps, might finish up as a good meal for the sharks.

We flew on, and I changed course in an attempt to follow the guidelines laid down by the controller before he faded from my R/T. I thought this operation analogous to finding a needle in a haystack. My main preoccupation was by now devoted to keeping a careful eye on my fuel gauges. But, all of a sudden, Bob Large – who had excellent vision, which I didn't – rang up.

'I see aircraft at our height, two o'clock, slightly high,' he reported over the R/T.

'OK,' I replied. 'Lead on until I see them.'

He opened his throttle and I maintained loose formation on him. After half a minute, I saw a number of black dots before my eyes.

'I see them,' I told Bob. 'Form formation line astern, keep it close. Put your gun-button on Fire, make sure your gunsight is well and truly on. Follow me. Act independently when we get split up.'

'Message received and understood,' Bob replied. Then he vanished from my sight while I was peering at the black dots which grew more and more discernible every moment.

'Buster,' I said over the R/T, meaning I was breaking the seals on my throttle quadrant, giving the Merlin emergency boost.

Black smoke poured from the exhausts as she swiftly

accelerated and the Merlin shuddered under the strains. We closed range to about a mile, and I recognized three Heinkels 111, covered by six Messerschmitts 109 swarming around like bees to their queen.

'We'll never get the bombers,' I told Bob Large over the R/T. 'Don't attempt to attack the bombers. Watch out for the fighters. Going in to the attack. Set course for base if it gets too hot.'

I dived towards the bombers, the Merlin still shuddering under emergency boost. As I expected, one of the Messerschmitts climbed towards me to fend off my attack. He was slow on the climb, but I throttled hard back, ducked under him and zoom-climbed after him. I hit him with my bullets, and saw his propeller come to a halt. He was a goner. I hauled round, and sure enough, there was another Me-109 coming up behind me. I kept the throttle shut down, which gave me a closer turning circle since I was at low speed by then, and pushed the throttle wide open as I came up behind him to gain acceleration. He was a sitting duck, and I watched my de Wilde incendiary bullets, mixed up with others, tracer and armour-piercing, throbbing into his engine. Black smoke belched, and I left the pilot to meet his Maker single-handed. Another idiot came into the attack, and I made short shrift of him and watched him explode into pieces of fire.

I made a quick search for the bombers, but the great sky gave me no indication as to their whereabouts. I was also mighty short of fuel, and it seemed that my two alternatives were to ditch in the Atlantic or force-land in a small Cornish field, with desperate stone walls surrounding it, which would not have been exactly of any assistance. In the event, I had sufficient gallons of 100-octane petrol left in my tanks to beat up the Droskyn Castle Hotel, and perform a couple of upward charlies, Fighter Command's personal signal that a victory could be claimed.

This brought 'Beau' driving to the airfield from the hotel to interrogate me as to how I saw the action. Bob Large landed shortly after me; I could not contact him on the R/T during or after the combat, and I was concerned as to his safety. I talked to him before 'Beau' arrived, and he told me that he had followed a Messerschmitt down, although it was belching black smoke. Before it hit the sea, he fired at it and saw it crash into the Atlantic. I told him that I would agree that we shared this kill. I didn't tell him that he was a bloody fool to follow down an obviously fatally stricken aircraft, because I was glad that he had not got himself mixed up in the vicious mêlée. I simply didn't want an inexperienced pilot under my custody when facing odds of nine to one. I was glad that he lost precious combat altitude, leaving me alone without the need to keep watch over his tail. The experience obviously did him no harm. Bob Large persuaded me to post him from No. 66 Squadron a few months later, to a squadron in No. 11 Group. He was granted a commission, survived the war with a DFC and bar sewn onto his tunic. Good for Bob. Thanks be to God, he followed down the Messerschmitt which I had disposed of, and thereby left me on my own to handle the situation as I thought fit.

Athol had another of his good ideas, and it actually worked. The trouble was that the Navy were trigger-happy. The captains of destroyers and frigates escorting the coastal convoys had a philosophy in their thick minds, one which could only have been dreamed up by simple sailors. This was to order their anti-aircraft gunners to shoot at *any* aircraft on sight. Their aircraft identification was so awful that they could not differentiate between friend or foe, so all aircraft were considered hostile. The fact that we were there for their protection, and that we were able to differentiate between friend and foe, passed straight through their tiny minds. Why, they would declare, a ship is more expensive than an aircraft and it contains more men, therefore let us take no risks. Which might have been all right for them, but I used to get fed up with being fired on by pom-poms when I was relieving one of our sections. I often thought of taking a pot-shot at the bridge of one ship or another – the gunners would not have hit me on a skidding attack, for their aiming was poor.

It was not possible for Athol to provide a pilot from the squadron to give lessons in aircraft recognition to the multifarious crews of the naval vessels, so he came to a better conclusion. He telephoned Admiralty House, Falmouth, and made an arrangement to visit the Naval Staff with half a dozen pilots from the squadron. Beforehand, he purloined a VHF R/T set from the squadron stores, and we drove to Falmouth with this radio transmitter/receiver. We met the assembled staff, sat around the table and conferred.

'I object,' Athol pronounced, 'to your gunners shooting at my aircraft. Not that it puts them in any danger because you couldn't hit a barn door at fifty yards' range. But if this practice continues, I fear that my pilots might exact retribution and dive-bomb your ships.'

'But surely they wouldn't do that!' the Admiral exclaimed. 'We can't have British aircraft bombing our ships!'

'Nor can we have British naval ships firing at British fighter aircraft, deployed in the air in your defence,' Athol replied grimly.

'Do you have a suggestion?' the Admiral asked.

'Yes,' Athol replied. And he produced from the case by his side a VHF R/T set. 'Put that in your flotilla leader's ship. My Signals NCO will explain to your signals officer how to tune it aboard ship. Then let's have a trial run in ship-to-aircraft communication. In the first place we would announce our identity when we were approaching your convoys. Added to which, normally two aircraft cover your convoys and contain two pilots; meaning that we in the air have two pairs of eyes to watch for approaching German aircraft. Each one of your ships has so many lookouts, so you've got a couple of hundred pairs of eyes who could give us warning of the approach of unidentified aircraft. This would ease our task no end – a kind of mutual benefit society.'

The Admiral ageed to lay on facilities for the technician

and the scheme was agreed. We then drank to its success.

The orgy lasted for several hours, and when night fell we decided to return to base. Before doing so, having been bidden a fond farewell by our Naval colleagues, we crept back to Admiralty House. Outside were two brass cannon, the pride and joy of the Admiral. Somehow or other we manhandled one into the Naval lorry and drove off in the dead of night. We not only pinched the lorry, we also stole the prized cannon. Needless to say, we had to return both items in the course of time.

Our ship-to-aircraft communications worked very well. The Admiralty ordered a crash programme to have all their ships fitted with such communications. If Athol hadn't proved the feasibility on a small and primitive scale, it would have taken the brass-hats a couple of years to work out the absolute necessity for themselves.

We were given cannon-firing Spitfires in the course of time, but we were not allowed to test the cannon because not enough cannon-shells were being produced. After a couple of weeks, I decided to test the cannon despite the vigorous protests of the Senior Armament Officer at our Sector Station. I flew out to a rock twenty miles out to sea from Perranporth, dived at it and fired my cannon. One shell emerged from each of the cannon, and then the guns jammed solid. It gave the sea-birds happily copulating on the rock a fright, but it gave me an even greater scare. We had been flying non-operational Spitfires for far too long. I tried again with another Spitfire and the same thing happened. Our Senior Armament NCO then gave the cannon a thorough inspection, and found that they were not properly machined.

Within two days the offending Spitfires were flown away, and we were re-equipped with 'long-range' Spitfires Mk 2. These aircraft had one thirty-gallon petrol tank slung under one wing, intended for ferry purposes, which would be removed for operations. The external tank increased the torque on take-off, and it also made us vulnerable when under attack by German aircraft. If it came to the point of belly-landing one of these marques, then there was a definite hazard in terms of sparks igniting either the petrol or the fumes in the tank, and causing the Spitfire to explode. Worse, even; the Messerschmitts now were each equipped with two 20-mm cannon and were new from the production lines, whereas our Spitfires had been flown for far too many hours for aircraft safety – metal fatigue, etc. – and were equipped with eight light machine-guns.

But, we were told, we would fly our 'long-range' Spitfires operationally with the cumbersome fuel tank hung beneath the wing. This, the Air Staff explained, was a war-winning weapons system. I told them to go and visit their psychiatrists. The Air Officer Commanding, Fighter Command was by now Sholto-Douglas, large, robust and the spitting image of Hermann Goering. He was flown down to the very west of Britain to inspect his war-winning system. I was in charge of the squadron, I can't remember why.

'Here we have the new war-winning system,' I explained to him, pointing at one of our monstrosities.

'But you can't be allowed to fly these bloody things operationally!' Sholto said, hair standing on end.

'Ours not to reason why, sir,' I replied. 'Into the Valley of Death and all that.'

'I'll see what I can do about it,' he told me after he had imbibed a few gins and tonics at the bar.

He was flown off in a cloud of dust. Nothing happened. We had to fly these strictly non-operational aircraft in combat.

Two other unfortunate squadrons were equipped with 'long-range' Spitfires, and I believe that all three squadrons were based in 10 Group.

Someone in East Anglia with apparently plenty of Blenheim light bombers on his hands would make requests, day after day, for Brand to dispatch his long-range Spitfires to East Anglia. We would take off in the afternoons, land at fighter stations such as Coltishall or Horsham St Faith, and

Athol would fix H-hour with the Blenheim leader via our ops room and the bomber bases, which were further inland. We would rendezvous with the Blenheim squadrons in the air at dawn next day, and they would break up into two flights. Athol would order me to escort one formation of bombers, and he would depart leading a flight escorting the other formation. The intention was that one of the flight of bombers would approach the coast of South Holland and sweep to the north searching for coastal convoys. The other flight would arrive at the northerly coast of Holland, and sweep on a southerly course on a similar search and destroy mission.

Our role was entirely confined to anti-fighter escort, ward off or destroy German Messerschmitts if they attempted to intercept the bombers. The Blenheims' role was to bomb ships in the convoys with 500-lb. bombs. There was so much wrong with this air plan as to make the mind boggle. In the first place, were these coastal convoys worthy of the attention of expensive aircraft, and even more expensive aircrew? Had anyone computed that? Next, was it prudent to dispatch our primitive Spitfires over a couple of hundred miles of the cold North Sea, where the failure of our Merlins would have killed us, either on impact or from exposure if we had been fortunate enough to rise to the surface and float with the aid of our Mae Wests? Was it prudent to put our antiquated Spitfires in the line of modern cannon-firing German fighters, when we were at the extremity of our range, and they were based a few miles from the scene of action? Fortunately for us, however, the Germans scarcely bothered to scramble their fighters to intercept these formations of British aircraft. They relied instead on flak-ships, interposed among the coastal merchant-shipping which comprised the convoys. German flak was one of the most deadly weapons in the German armoury, whether ground-based or ship-borne. Whereas the British, for historical reasons too boring to describe, always tended to consider ack-ack as second-rate, which it was almost throughout the war, because of the apathy underlying it.

Furthermore, the Blenheim captains were ordered to *bomb* shipping on a straight and level approach, keeping low over the water – an impossible stipulation. Dive-bombing might have brought success but the Blenheim was not designed in that role. Torpedo-bombing would have made sense – the two great British capital ships, *Prince of Wales* and *Repulse*, were crippled by Japanese aerial torpedoes, but the Blenheims were not equipped to carry torpedoes. The Blenheims suffered accordingly. Of the six bombers I escorted on each of these raids, I believe that four were shot down while making their attacks – and by flak-ships. It was a murder of the innocents. And I do not remember one of their bombs even gaining so much as a near miss on a ship, certainly not a direct hit.

The turnover rate of Blenheim aircrew was positively satanic. On each mission, assuming shipping was sighted, and it normally was, fifty per cent of the aircrew engaged were shot down. It was not unknown for a sergeant pilot with the Blenheims to be promoted squadron commander, within a year. This was so because he would have been the only member of aircrew to survive this murderous, lunatic holocaust. Even today, nearly forty years on, a Royal Commission should be convened to judge on this tragic comedy.

Ignore death, up to the last moment; then, when it can't be ignored any longer, have yourself squirted full of morphia and shuffle off in a coma. But the trouble was, the Blenheim aircrews did not carry morphia.

11

The Changing Face of Clickety-Click

By the spring of 1941 No. 66 Squadron's complement was
changing rapidly. Pilot changes were more frequent than
among the ground crews, and we were fortunate enough to
retain some of our stalwart fitters and riggers who had been
with us since I joined the squadron. Bobby Oxspring was
posted away for a rest from operations which, although it
left me as the senior flight commander and deputy squadron
commander, was a sad loss, for Bobby was the longest-
serving pilot on the squadron and a very experienced fighter
pilot. He and I had been in action on more than one occasion
when we had flattened the opposition.

Bobby was a Yorkshire man and proud of it, quite tall,
broad, very tough, with fair curly hair. He always seemed to
have a grin on his face, though at times I wondered what he
found so funny about life. He had taken me along on his
wing on several training flights while I was an apprentice on
the squadron, and he was a natural pilot. He certainly did
mortal damage to a number of aircraft during the Battle of
Britain and beyond. We were more than good friends; we
were colleagues, having served as joint flight commanders
for several months.

Before he left, Bobby took me to a pub for a drink, and as I
remember it, we finished up in a ditch, upside down in his
car. It is not difficult to escape from a car lying on its roof. A
couple of tough young men could normally heave it right
side up and, assuming it was roadworthy, it could be driven
back to our fighter base. Our blacksmiths were also expert at
panel bashing, and our paint-shops were manned by efficient
sprayers of paint. They could work miracles on a damaged
car, and they frequently did.

Then Pickering was posted away, only to meet his death in

a flying accident a few weeks later. As rookie pilots joined to replace those posted from us, the nature of the squadron began to alter dramatically. Two Free French officers arrived, one of them an aristo, a one-time test-pilot, the other a tough commissioned NCO pilot in the French Air Force who had been awarded the equivalent of our VC. The aristo almost invariably had a French cigarette hanging limply in his lips stinking the room out. The other firmly smoked a pipe. I was young and innocent when I took command of No. 66 Squadron, so I allocated these French officers a single room – as the establishment of officers on the squadron increased, it became necessary for bedrooms to contain two officers. As 'captain of the ship' I, of course, had my own bedroom. One evening I was wandering along the corridor and from their room I heard blue murder and French curses. I opened the door and found them struggling on the floor attempting to kill each other. I managed to separate them. Capitaine Claisse, the aristo, spoke broken English; his compatriot had no English.

'Was it an *affaire du coeur*?' I inquired, keeping them apart with difficulty.

'*Merde! Non! Le bâtard, c'est un sâle Vichyite! Moi, je suis Gaulliste! Pissez sur son visage!*'

I put my arms round their shoulders.

'*Accompagnez-moi au direction du bar*,' I instructed. 'We'll sort this bloody nonsense out amicably.'

We never sorted it out. Never get involved in French politics. The French *ne se servent de la pensée que pour autoriser leurs injustices, et n'emploient les paroles que pour déguiser leurs pensées*.

We had to slide the commissioned NCO over to another squadron, but we kept the aristo on and made him a flight commander, *pour encourager les autres*. He was a nice guy to have around, but his deputy effectively ran his flight for him.

But what you lose on the swings you gain on the roundabouts. Pilot Officer P. B. (Laddie) Lucas suddenly turned up as a new entry, and I immediately grabbed him to join my flight. He had learned to fly in Canada and had been held up in Iceland; he had of course no combat experience. He was immaculately dressed, polite, co-operative, but under his modest exterior I was shrewd enough to see the warning signs of a born leader of men, although he was about five years older than I. He was eager to learn and always co-operative, a great asset to a squadron which was swiftly losing out in terms of the calibre and quality of its officers.

Laddie had been an infant prodigy in that he lived near that fine golf-course at Sandwich and was born, so to speak, with a left-handed golf club in his hand. He became the longest left-handed driver at golf in the country, captained his school team, captained Cambridge University and was, I believe, Captain of the British Ryder Cup team. He was much too modest to blurt out such information, but I vaguely remembered his name as golfing correspondent to the Beaverbrook Press.

So far as possible I endeavoured to fly Laddie in my section of two or four aircraft. His potential, I felt, was too great for him to be knocked off through inadequate leadership in the air until he had really found his wings. I was rather like an eagle fussing over its eaglet, but it paid off in the end. (Anyway, Laddie had scored enough 'eagles' on the famous golf-courses around the world, so he was quite used to the breed.)

Whereas when I joined Clickety-Click it was very much an English squadron – apart from the odd Scot and Irishman – now, in early 1941, it was quickly becoming a Commonwealth squadron, and the English were certainly in the minority among the pilots. Australian pilot officers and sergeant pilots arrived, as did New Zealanders, South Africans and Canadians. The Australians wore their own dark-blue uniforms, but the others wore RAF uniforms with their nationality sewn on the outside of the shoulders of their tunics and battledress. They were in the main rookies, and the hard core of operational – even flying – experience rested very much on Athol's shoulders and my own. It was even getting difficult for us to detail section leaders for the mundane tasks of escorting convoys. Whereas pilots on the eastern flank of 10 Group, and in 11 Group, were either quick or dead on their sweeps against the Luftwaffe over France. Experience could be swiftly obtained in those regions, but not in Cornwall.

The futile sweeps by Blenheims over Dutch coastal waters were dying out, as more and more bombers were destroyed by flak, and more and more aircrews bit the dust. However, someone or other decided to make a grandiose and quite useless gesture, presumably intended to remove the remaining Blenheims from the face of the earth. This was to order the crews of some fifty Blenheims to attack a power station on the German border. Consequently, No. 66 Squadron, among other 'long-range' units, was ordered to deploy to an East Anglian airfield, take off at dawn the next day, and escort the Blenheim force back from Antwerp. Since we had not the slightest hope of making landfall at Antwerp, flying over the sea, relying on our compasses, having no knowledge of the variable winds over the sea, having no sextants or any other form of navigation worth discussing, it was decided that a single Blenheim would lead us to Antwerp and then fly with all haste for home.

By this time, officers in the post of 'wing leaders' had been established. Such people were, in effect, air advisers to the sector commanders; and if formations of wing strength were detailed to fly on operations, it was axiomatic that they would lead the three squadrons involved. Our wing leader was based at our sector station at Portreath, and he was a good officer but unfortunately his combat experience was negligible. He had previously been a flying instructor, and there is as much difference between a pilot skilled in the arts of flying instruction and fighter combat as there is between the Great Pyramid of Gizeh and the gentlemen's lavatory at Waterloo Station. However, due to his senior rank as wing commander, compared with Athol's status as squadron leader and mine as flight lieutenant, we both had to come under his operational command when wing formations of two or three squadrons were flown.

A funny thing about the Royal Air Force was that we were often ordered to fly on operations in formations that had never been practised in non-combat exercises. Thus Dowding ordered wing formations consisting of four squadrons grouped together over Dunkirk, but we had never flown wing formations of as much as two squadrons on exercises. Similarly, although our wing leader at Portreath was ordered to lead three 'long-range' squadrons of Spitfires to Antwerp, to my knowledge he had never led a Spitfire squadron in his life. Indeed, I remember giving him his first 'operational' – hardly combat – flight, when he stayed positioned on my starboard wing while we patrolled a convoy. It was not his fault, of course, that he should be handed responsibility for handling a wing tactically over enemy territory when he had not the slightest knowledge of what he was about. That was entirely the responsibility of those in the Air Ministry who selected him for his appointment.

We arrived at Coltishall at dusk, met our opposite numbers who would fly their squadron aircraft to Antwerp, and the wing leader, together with Athol and the other squadron commanders, talked to the captain of the Blenheim which would navigate us to Antwerp. H-hour was set when the leader of the main force of Blenheims would hopefully arrive over Antwerp after making his raid, to set course for England, home and beauty. We were to fly to Antwerp a couple of hundred feet over the sea, nice and low to avoid German radar detection with our navigator in the lead. R/T silence was to be strictly enforced, and as we saw the Belgian coast on the horizon, I noted that the wing had fallen too far behind our Blenheim for safety. I could hardly press my R/T transmit button and tell the wing leader to close right up behind our navigating Blenheim, else I would have blown the gaff to the German Y Service. They would have scrambled a couple of wings of Messerschmitts, and as the force of bombers returning from the raid were at low level and optimistically outside the ken of German radars, the Messerschmitts might have bounced them and destroyed the lot. (There was nothing very difficult about shooting down a Blenheim, which was a useless aircraft in all its designated roles.)

I saw a black spot in the distance which quickly materialized as a Messerschmitt 109, heading straight for the Blenheim at high speed. We were about a mile behind our navigating aircraft, and powerless to give it any assistance. I saw smoke issue from the cannon ports of the Me-109, and the Blenheim immediately blew up in thick fiery pieces of duralumin, in which were mixed the remnants of human bodies. It was about the finest example of fixed-gun firing I had ever witnessed, but it also represented a complete let-down, for thirty-six Spitfires were close – but not close enough – behind the Blenheim.

The only method of air-to-air communication the old Royal Flying Corps had was hand signals. We were also trained in signalling by hand, in case of R/T failure, or the need for R/T silence. I can give a few examples. With two pilots flying in close formation on your wing, you would clench your fist and pretend to beat the back of your flying helmet with vigour; this meant form section line-astern. If you pointed your hand daintily to the right, that meant aircraft echelon starboard. If you thought your aircraft had become unserviceable in the air, you would waggle your wings vigorously, and point your finger down. If you wanted your Number Two to take over the lead of the flight or section, you would point vigorously at him and then screw your hand around indicating that you were leaving the formation and ordering your Number Two to take the lead. It sounds complicated but it wasn't.

When I saw our navigating Blenheim blow up, I pointed vigorously at my Number Two, screwed my hand round, slapped open the throttle, climbed away from my flight, and peeled off in a screaming dive. The offending Messerschmitt pilot had swept below the Spitfire wing after his head-on attack, and made a right turn for Belgium. He was a couple of miles away from me when I got on his tail, and I broke the throttle seals to gain maximum boost; but he did likewise, meaning that I was only catching up on him slowly. He led me a dance over the flat landscape of Belgium, and I soon appreciated that I could not maintain emergency throttle for much longer, else my Merlin would break up under the strain or I would run out of fuel. So I decided to haul round on a reciprocal course and flew low towards the Belgian coast, skidding my way along to avoid being hit by flak.

When I was over the sea, I felt safe and throttled back to conserve fuel. But a sharp look in my mirror showed that this crack German pilot was on my tail about 2,000 yards away, but catching up fast. I saw a small cumulus cloud, climbed towards it like a bat out of hell, turned at four gee inside it and came out on the German's tail. I was long in range, but gave him a long burst and saw strikes on his fuselage. Then I set course on a heading of 270 degrees and nursed the Merlin back to East Anglia. I hope I killed that expert, audacious, German pilot, but I doubt that I did.

Part of the joys of Perranporth revolved around birds. There were seagulls in profusion and they laid a great many eggs. All that was required was for a few of us to clamber a hundred feet or so down the cliffs, preferably with safety-ropes tied round us and carrying suitable containers. On a few such sorties we could collect an enormous number of eggs, a welcome addition to wartime rations. They were large, succulent, but tasted somewhat of fish. Taken in moderation they certainly enhanced our diet. Plovers' eggs, of course, were rarer and more difficult to find, but they were well worth the search. However, birds were a definite hazard to aircraft when taking off and landing, as I can vouch.

When I was detailed to fly on navigational exercise at high level during my advanced flying training, I didn't; I flew at ground level just for the fun of it. I heard an almighty bang, and my Harvard positively shuddered. The controls went slightly awry, and I noticed blood on the leading wing. I landed in due course, and reported to my instructor that it appeared that I had struck a bird, high in the sky. He walked out to my aircraft, took due note of the gaping hole in the wing, put his hand into the hole and fished around. He hauled out the remains of a chicken.

'At what height did you hit this chicken?' he inquired.

My brain worked like fury.

'Shortly before I levelled out for landing,' I lied.

He gazed at me suspiciously.

'I know of no chicken farms on our landing approach,' he said sternly.

'Nor did I until I hit the bloody chicken,' I replied.

'But a chicken can only jump a couple of feet in the air,' he persisted. 'You must have been stinking low on your approach.'

'Not impossible, sir,' I replied. 'But then as you know only too well I am a stinking awful pilot.'

He grinned and let me off the hook. In fact I hit the chicken when I was flying at about two feet, at full speed, on a 'high-level' navigational flight.

Twenty-five years later, flying a Canberra bomber at dusk, over friendly German airspace, my aircraft rocked as it struck a flying object. The nose canopy was splintered, the Air Speed Indicator pilot-head was bent and I no longer knew what my flying speed was in flight or, even worse, for the final approach and landing. I managed to put the aircraft on the runway in one piece, and the ground crews then found that I had collided with an eagle. What a mess it made!

Birds were a definite hazard to aircraft at Perranporth and some strange department of the Air Ministry decided that they should send down falcons together with handlers to keep the airspace over the airfield clear. There were two snags to this concept of operations. First, British agents and members of the Maquis in France tended to use homing pigeons for their communications network, and the falcons used to kill them with deadly rapidity and eat the all-important messages attached to them. Next, our aircraft tended to land with large holes in their fuselage because they had collided with the falcons in mid-air. So then the edict was reversed, and we were ordered to shoot hawks and falcons if they got in range. We did no such thing. In fact we had a pet buzzard which one of our pilots, a keen ornithologist, found with an injured wing. He had a large coop made for it, and we would feed it with rabbit meat and suchlike. When its wing healed we gave it its freedom – but it still visited us because it knew how to get free food without hunting for it.

Apart from the strong winds with which we often had to cope in Cornwall, there was another dangerous aspect to the weather factor at Perranporth – sea-fog. Fog normally occurs in periods of slack winds, but sea-fog can occur at almost all times. I once flew when I was drunk; well, perhaps not drunk, but I had certainly imbibed strong drink. It happened when I was over a convoy with my Number Two and the controller rang up and informed me that the general area around Perranporth had suddenly become covered with fog, and that I had better land elsewhere pretty bloody fast. Where could I divert to, I inquired.

'No idea, old boy,' he replied. 'There seems to be fog encroaching over the whole of the south-west of England.'

'Supposing I bail out?' I suggested tentatively. 'I imagine that you've placed all the air-sea rescue services at immediate readiness.'

'Oh Lord! I never thought of that,' he said remorsefully. 'Ah! But even if I had, the rescue ships couldn't see where they were going because of the fog.'

'You,' I replied firmly, 'are in urgent need of psychiatric attention. I am abandoning this convoy and will make a diversionary landing. Out!'

I called my Number Two into close formation and headed for Plymouth; we had just about sufficient petrol aboard to get there. Fog was slipping in fast as we made landfall, but I spotted a small airfield which would not be obliterated by fog for a further three minutes. I checked the wind-sock, ordered my Number Two to get in close, and told him to land in tight formation on my wing. The airfield was short and had no

runways, but we skidded to a halt without breaking the
perimeter wire, turned, taxied in and parked on the grass by
the main buildings where I saw a White Ensign flapping in the
breeze. A posse of naval officers and ratings surrounded us –
they had never seen a Spitfire at close quarters before, let
alone two Spitfires.

'Welcome aboard,' a naval lieutenant yelled as I climbed
out of my cockpit, giving me a traditional salute although I
held the same equivalent rank as he did. (It's all part of the
protocol.)

'Nice to be aboard your ship,' I replied. (It wasn't a ship, it
was an airfield, but the Navy always like to think they are
aboard ship even when they are on dry land.) 'Have you got a
bowser filled with 100-octane petrol?'

'Petty officer,' he snarled. 'Get a bowser here filled with
100-octane petrol, I don't care how you achieve it, but *do* it.'

'Aye, aye, sir,' the petty officer replied, and rushed off into
the distance with a gang of men. I expect they pinched the
bowser from the nearest Shell depot, but it arrived in quick
time. My Number Two and I borrowed screwdrivers and
similar items and oversaw the refuelling of the Spitfires, by
which time the airfield was thick with fog, visibility about ten
yards.

'Sorry about this,' I said. 'But we will have to hang around
until the fog clears. Can you put us up in your mess for the time
being?'

'Mess?' the naval lieutenant frowned. 'Oh, you mean our
wardroom, don't you?'

'Sorry,' I replied. 'Of course I meant your wardroom. And
I'd like to visit the heads some time.'

'You mean the lavatory?'

'No. I mean the heads.' (When in Rome try and look like a
Roman.)

'But of course. Incidentally, we are having a party tonight.
Like to join in?'

'That's most kind, but we are scarcely equipped to go to a
party.'

We'd been flying in shirt-sleeves, with Mae Wests, and wore flying boots.

'Not to worry. We will lend you tunics – naval, of course.'

'Thanks very much.'

'Well, let's go to the bar and tank up ahead of the party. We've got smashing WRNS here. Their busts ought to be exhibited in the Louvre or somewhere.'

'Could I be the judge of that? I am expert on busts and also the Louvre.'

'Of course,' he replied. 'Nice to have a connoisseur around.'

He was quite right about the quality of the busts, and for that matter the WRNS. My Number Two and I, both wearing naval tunics over our RAF trousers, quaffed a couple of double scotches while courting the WRNS, then my mistaken sense of duty overcame me.

'Can I use your telephone?' I asked our host.

I rang up Perranporth, and was told that the fog had cleared, but it would be returning in about half an hour.

'Thanks very much,' I said to our bewildered host. 'We're taking off.'

'It's a bit misty outside,' he commented.

'I'm a bit misty inside,' I told him. 'Get hold of a few ratings to remove the chocks and things like that.'

We flung our naval tunics on the bar, tied on our Mae Wests, and sprinted for our Spitfires. We got the propellers turning, waved the chocks away, taxied to the upwind end of the airfield and roared into the air. I put my oxygen supply onto emergency flow which, combined with the several whiskies I had downed, positively made me inebriated. I led my Number Two practically at sea level. I kept making the attempt to strike the Atlantic rollers a glancing blow with my propeller, but fortunately did not quite make impact. When Perranporth airfield loomed up, fog was already creeping over the downwind end of the runway.

'Land immediately,' I told my Number Two. I watched him touch down.

Then I made a split-arse turn, lowering my undercarriage

and flaps simultaneously on the turn, and straightened out with the threshold of the runway dead ahead. I touched down and almost immediately ran into thick fog. There were no runway lights, but I managed to keep on the runway through instinct. When I braked to a halt, it was impossible to taxi the Spitfire. Visibility was nil. I stopped the engine, clambered out of the cockpit, and attempted to find my way to the squadron dispersal. It was impossible. I kept walking in great circles, and inevitably returned to my Spitfire as it loomed up only a few yards from the extremity of my vision. Eventually I decided to climb aboard. Then I closed the cockpit canopy and fell asleep. I remained in the Spitfire for the whole of the night.

Next morning, the fog had abated and the ambulance and fire-engines managed to locate the aircraft at the end of the runway. Nevertheless, I walked in an absolutely straight line across the grass to the squadron dispersal.

You've got to be young to be lucky – *virginibus puerisque*.

12

Squadron Commander

Much to his chagrin, Athol Forbes was promoted out of his command of No. 66 Squadron in the early summer of 1941 and sent to hold down a staff appointment at Headquarters, No. 10 Group, based in a country house at Box, not far from Bath. He must have recommended that I should be given command of the squadron, and Jack Boret, our Sector Commander, placed his thumbprint on the recommendation.

On the eve of his departure, Athol took me to the local five-star hotel, The Tregenna Castle, owned by the Great Western Railway. Anything less like a modern British Rail hotel would be hard to imagine. The decor was sumptuous, the food superb, and the wine most drinkable. Athol and I over-indulged ourselves in everything, including some of the attractive female guests, but more especially the wine. He drove the squadron commander's Humber saloon, which had been patched up on many occasions by our blacksmiths and panel-bashers, to the hotel. On our return, he rather overdid things and knocked down a few stone walls 'protecting' the sides of the lanes. However, we sent him off with a driver to Box the next morning, sitting in another Humber which we hijacked from the Sector Station at Portreath.

After I left No. 66 Squadron I went on to command more Fighter Command squadrons: No. 1 Squadron which I commanded was clearly the senior squadron in the RAF, and it was a great squadron in RAF history. I positively gloried in having command of No. 43 but, curiously, No. 1 left me cold. But whereas I was appointed to command Nos 1 and 43 and and another two squadrons, wearing the stripes on the sleeves of my RAF tunic which indicated that I held 'field' rank, as they say in the army, No. 66 Squadron was something quite different. I had joined it as a bog-rat, passed my operational apprenticeship in it, commanded one of the two flights, and then was fortunate enough to become the squadron commander. It can be summed up, I suppose, in terms of sweet and painful nostalgia. And, of course, I had the tremendous advantage of having as my commanders two great men, Rupert Leigh and Athol Forbes; they don't make them like that these days. I was the lowest form of life in the RAF, and they were both men about town. But they nurtured me, they succoured me; they were certainly my tutors, unlike my university professors who have totally faded from my memory. 'Better be born lucky than rich.'

So it occurred that my first problem as the new squadron commander was to work on the problem of my official car. I showed it to our senior blacksmith.

'How long will it take you to put this back in one piece, Smithie?' I inquired.

He removed his RAF forage-cap, scratched his hair, had a quick look and gazed at me with a perplexed look in his eye.

'Cor, bleeding hell, sir,' he replied. 'If I put the whole of my team onto it, I might get it fixed up within six months. But, of course, you wouldn't get any panel-bashing done on the Spitfires in that period of time.'

I thought for a moment. Difficulties are there, after all, only to be solved.

'Get your gang together after nightfall, Smithie, and we'll push the bleeding car over the cliff.'

'Is that an order, sir?' he asked.

'Yes. H-hour is 2200 hours. Rendezvous by the car. Discretion is the watchword. All personnel to keep their mouths shut.'

We met at H-hour, by which time a minor hurricane was blowing. I switched on the headlights, which by some freak of fortune worked, released the handbrake and cautiously allowed the Humber to roll slowly down the slope. I brought it to a halt just before the gradient hit one-in-two and led on to a vertical drop into the sea, a couple of hundred feet ahead. The posse padded after me. It was reminiscent of eighteenth-century smugglers getting up to their nefarious deeds. I disembarked, left the driver's door open, and told the gang to shove like hell when I said 'Go'. I released the handbrake, said 'Go', and they gave the car a shove. It rumbled like a hearse on its way to a crematorium, headlights flashing up and down as it bounced over rocks and things. Then it reared up on its back wheels, gave a kind of sigh, and fell vertically, nigh on 300 feet, into the tempestuous seas.

The next day I telephoned the Officer i/c Motor Transport at Portreath.

'George,' I said, 'I want another Humber.'

'So does the Sector Commander,' he bleated.

'Why? What's wrong with his?'

'He says that because it's done 30,000 miles, it isn't prestigious enough for his rank and status any longer. Anyway I've got only one new Humber in reserve, and if I indent for another, Group will want to know why, and I haven't got any good reason. In any case, why do you want another car? My records show that the No. 66 Squadron Commander's car has only done about 35,000 miles. They are supposed to last for 80,000 miles, you know, before we strip them and put them together again.'

'Funny thing happened last night, George,' I said.

'What?' he inquired suspiciously.

'My Humber blew off the cliff. It's in the sea, or halfway to America.'

'What!' he screeched. 'Didn't you have the brakes on?'

'Oh, yes. But the wind caught it broadside-on and rolled it down the cliffs. I'll show you the exact spot where it happened if you like. On the other hand,' I went on brightly, 'this unfortunate accident has solved your problem. All you have to do is to give the Sector Commander a new Humber, let me have his part-worn one and indent for a new car. Put on the indent form that my car was destroyed by an act of God.'

'All right,' he grumbled. 'Send a driver down this afternoon and he can pick up the Sector Commander's car.'

So that was that, a good compromise. In any case, Athol had pranged the car on so many occasions that it was positively dangerous.

Not long afterwards we had a real hurricane which blew down the marquee used as a rest-room and ops centre for the pilots. Four pilots were asleep in their beds at fifteen minutes' available for night interceptions. They were not only blown from their beds, they were nearly blown over the cliff.

Now, apart from the swiftly changing character of Clickety-Click due to the old-timers being sent away as instructors and rookies taking their places, a further change occurred because I, the new squadron commander, had not yet seen my twenty-second birthday; whereas both Rupert and Athol had by now celebrated their thirtieth birthdays. Whereas they were men of sound judgment, full of commonsense, adults, I was a kid not long out of university.

A Camp Commandant proper was appointed before Athol left No. 66 Squadron, and he gave no trouble for Athol was, by the standards of the day, a senior squadron leader in the flying branch of the RAF. This other officer had been an observer in the Royal Flying Corps, had volunteered for active service in the Administrative Branch for the Second World War, and all in all was quite a nice man, if a little pernickety for my liking. I was a substantive flying officer, acting flight lieutenant, now given command of the squadron in the acting rank of squadron leader. So old Bubble-guts, as I used to call the Camp Commandant, thought he would pull seniority on me, thus forgetting that in the liquid dew of youth contagious blastments are most imminent. So I was most rude to him and told him to look after the lavatories while I looked after the airfield and my squadron. Not unnaturally when our pilots' marquee blew down, therefore, he was most unco-operative in attempting to find us alternative accommodation. So I promptly declared No. 66 Squadron non-operational until further notice in a Top Secret signal to the Sector Commander at Portreath with copies to Group and Fighter Command HQ.

Within two days we had a firmly embedded pilots' dispersal hut, and an insulated parachute hanging tower.

Now and again it was necessary to act tough, and Bubble-guts and I co-operated from then on over the operational effectiveness of my squadron. I am rather like a Gurkha. Those little soldiers of Nepal will march to hell under the leadership of officers they respect and admire. I would con-form to the utmost when my boss showed high qualities of leadership in all senses of the word, which includes a high level of intellect. But I gained a reputation as a noncon-formist, simply because all too few senior officers in the RAF came up to the standards I expected of them. As W. H. Auden said: 'Only those in the last stage of disease could believe that children are true judges of character', and I believe him. I also believe that more often than not dogs are true judges of character. It seems that I must be a Gurkha, a child, or a dog.

I was constantly having rows with fighter controllers and, indeed, when my flying career extended into the jet age, I was constantly having rows with air traffic controllers when they put a foot wrong. To them, if they did something totally insane it amounted to a small error of judgment. To me, it was more often than not a matter of life or death. In the summer of 1941 we were having considerable difficulty with the 'Milk Train'. This took the form of a German aircraft, either a Dornier long-range flying boat or a souped-up Junkers with long-range tanks. Regular as clockwork, these aircraft would appear on the radar screens, flying beyond our range, roaming the inshore Atlantic and taking note of the weather prospects. Britain's weather is normally dependent on meteorological conditions in the Atlantic and, having no weather ships and similar devices, the Luftwaffe were short of information as to weather prospects for the British and German bomber raids planned that night. Time and time again we would scramble sections of fighters at dawn, when the radars gave us information that the Milk Train was entering our operational fighter sector. Time and again we had to return to base without firing our guns, because the target was well outside our radius of action.

In the same manner that I used to fly low over the Channel Islands when based on Exeter, I adopted a similar policy with the Scilly Isles. The Scillies, unlike the Channel Islands, were not under German occupation, and as I waggled my wings over the islands, displayed RAF roundels, and generally showed the flag to boost the morale of the inhabitants, I struck a good idea. Why not establish a small airstrip on St Mary's, the largest of the islands, and base a couple of sections of my Spitfires there, not only in defence of the islands – which were outrageously vulnerable to air attack by the Luftwaffe – but also to intercept the Milk Train, which was of great importance to the German meteorologists? With the added radius of action provided by having aircraft on such a forward base, we could catch Fritz with his pants down.

There were few difficulties to the plan. We would need a primitive runway of pierced steel planking (PSP) on some ground, level for about 700 yards. The hotels and guest houses could be used as the billets for the dozen or so pilots and airmen required. Underwater telephone lines were already in existence, and one of them could easily be transformed into a scrambled hot line. Aircraft which went unserviceable operationally, but were in flying condition, could be flown back to Perranporth when relief aircraft would be flown out. Small ships could transport sufficient essential spares, such as VHF radios, sparking plugs, spare Merlins with a crane to install them, new tyres and so on. We would need camouflage netting for our Spitfires, because we would not want the Luftwaffe to appreciate that their all-essential Milk Train was in dire danger.

The whole thing was obvious to me, and it was an essential operational requirement. I wrote a brief plan and showed it to Jack Boret, our Sector Commander. He read it, and his wicked eyes pierced mine: 'I will forward it with my strong endorsement,' he said.

Nothing happened, of course. But if we had fixed the Milk Train, a great number of our major cities and ports would not necessarily have been blown up.

Early one morning before the dawn was rising, I lay asleep on my bed dreaming of sweet nothings, although I probably had in mind the truism that if you kiss the mistress you cannot kiss the maid. But I was almost certainly wondering whether or not the maid might be better in bed than the mistress. Then a grimy hand shook me by the shoulder and roared in my tired ear, 'Bleeding Ops want to talk to you sharp quick-like, sir.'

It was our bleary-eyed telephone orderly, Aircraftman Stroud, who was supposed to have been alert and ready alongside the operations telephone the whole night long, but who had been clearly kipping for the last several hours. When at night readiness we slept in our trousers and shirts, with our Mae Wests, gauntlets, flying helmets and parachutes within touching distance. I wandered to the telephone.

'I say!' said the controller with a burst of enthusiasm. 'The Milk Train is right of course. It is just approaching Land's End, well within our range. We've got it this time, don'tcherknow.'

'If any sod gets it, it will be me not you,' I replied scathingly. 'And have you looked out of the window, because I have!'

'Window, sir? We haven't got any windows. I am buried underground in the Ops Room. Our Met. officers say weather conditions are excellent.'

'Have they looked out of the bloody window?' I inquired acidly.

'Well, no. They are buried underground with me. But they assure me that their synoptic Met. charts are absolutely accurate. The sun is breaking through, and patches of fog will disperse very shortly. You must get a move on! You've got the Milk Train cold.'

'I happen to have looked out of the window,' I remarked. 'There is dense fog over the airfield which has lifted to about fifty feet. I will take off on my own, but on no account are you to order my Number Two to take off after me. You can't fly in this weather, but I am going to. Give me course and height on the bandit when I call you up after take-off.'

'But you can't fly on your own,' he protested. 'The book of rules ordains that there must be two pilots in formation. Interceptions by single aircraft are strictly out of court.'

'Damn the book of rules,' I told him. 'I will now scramble. You are under strict orders not to instruct another pilot to attempt to join up with me. I am signing off. Out.'

Whereupon I ran to my Spitfire strapping on my Mae West, while my fitter and rigger sprinted after me carrying my parachute and other accoutrements. They heaved me aboard and helped me to get the engine running. Cloud base was at about fifty feet, visibility a quarter of a mile. However, according to my predictions the weather would have improved, not deteriorated, when I was due to land. I raised my undercarriage at ten feet when in the air, kept the Spitfire at that height, and climbed sharply over the cliffs. I dropped her down almost to sea level, which gave me an effective cloud base of some 250 feet, climbed until I was skimming just below the layers of mist to extend my R/T radius of communication, and asked for further information on the bandit. The information the controller gave me, not surprisingly, was muffled and vague, but I changed course according to his directions.

It was virtually impossible to distinguish between the grey of the mist and the grey of the sea below, and I had to make constant references to my flight instruments to confirm that I wasn't flying in an inverted position. I was suddenly startled when I heard the voice of my Number Two faintly over the R/T, asking what my position was – as if I knew.

'What the hell do you think you are doing?' I snapped.

'The controller ordered me to scramble and make contact with you,' he replied faintly.

'You are to return to base immediately,' I told him. 'Turn seawards on a reciprocal heading. Reduce speed to 150 mph. Head for the land. When you see the cliffs to your starboard, keep them in visual range. Just ahead of Perranporth Bay you will see the Droskyn Castle Hotel. Put your flaps down, increase engine power and make a climbing turn to starboard. The runway will be dead ahead. Do not attempt to overshoot if you make a balls-up of the approach. Land on your belly if necessary. Is that clearly understood?'

'Message received and understood,' he replied. 'Am returning to base as instructed.'

My eyes were red with rage, which blurred my instrument panel. But my vision cleared after about five minutes. Then I saw the silhouette of a Junkers 88, skimming in and out of the misty sky. I dived to gain speed and opened the throttle, climbed gently and waited while scanning in the mist. I saw the aircraft for a brief, fleeting second, applied deflection and used up all my ammunition in a long burst of fire. Half the time I was firing I was guessing as to the location of the bomber. I saw red flashes, but they might have been spots in my eyes. I broke off the attack, throttled hard back, and made a gentle descent down to sea level. I kept the Spitfire flying slow at about 150 mph, and edged my way towards the land. I had to bank hard when I saw the cliffs loom out of the mist, followed the coastline until I dimly perceived Perranporth harbour. Then I edged her up, saw the runway dead ahead, put down full flaps and then selected undercarriage down. After landing, my spaniel, Pookie, was waiting as I came to a halt at the squadron dispersal. She had an anxious look on her face.

I rang up the controller, and what I said to him history will never record.

13

Beware We Strike

I always believed in squadron mascots, and our emblem was a rattlesnake poised to strike so I wrote to the London Zoo and asked them to send me a rattlesnake for my squadron. It might be a good idea, I suggested, if they first put their dentist onto the job of extracting its poisonous fangs before they put it on the train. They politely declined, so we had to make do with grass-snakes. One pilot picked up a viper in error, but someone trod on its head before it could get its fangs into its finder. However, grass-snakes were insidious creatures, so I found myself a bull-terrier to act as our squadron mascot. He grew into a very large white specimen of the breed with one brown patch over one eye, looking like a boxer after Muhammed Ali had given him a straight jab. Bull-terriers, be they conventionally bred or of the Staffordshire variety, are the toughest animal on four legs for their weight. I am constantly bemused why, to my knowledge, no RAF fighter squadron had made a bull-terrier its emblem. I called him 'Crippen' as I reckoned he would make a more effective murderer than Dr Henry Hawley Crippen – who wasn't very good at his job in fact. Crippen was looked after by me and my batman and grew in size and stature, and he eventually became the true squadron mascot. But he was careful with his tactics; he never had a fight until he was fully grown, which took about three years. Then he was attacked by a bull-mastiff and promptly strangled it to death, although he was severely wounded in the action. Someone painted a DFC on his chest for his gallantry.

Having had command of No. 66 Squadron for a month or so, I began to champ at the bit. Convoy patrols were boring and, in my view, futile. In short, we were wasting our time and doing very little to help the war effort. I worked out my

personal motto, which was: *'De l'audace, encore l'audace.'*
However, I was constrained by the dead hand of HQ No. 10
Group, and in theory had to retain the squadron in a
defensive, and not an offensive, posture. Nevertheless, I had
my eye on a German bomber base near Lannion on the Brest
Peninsula. I asked 'Beau' to discreetly get hold of a large-scale
map of the area, also a plan of the layout of the airfield. I kept
this material locked away when I was not making a detailed
study of it. My intention was to strafe it on a single-wave
attack, approaching from the south to surprise the flak
defences. There are about ten major principles of war,
dreamed up by von Clausewitz, and my two favourites were
offensive action coupled with surprise. According to the
intelligence people, the airfield was stacked with Junkers 88s,
which was an effective multi-role combat aircraft – bomber,
night fighter and reconnaissance vehicle. I didn't divulge my
innermost thoughts to anybody. If 10 Group HQ had got to
know what I was planning, they would have either given me
strict orders not to proceed, or tried to make their own plan
which would have resulted in a complete nonsense. My only
remedy was patience and it paid off.

One day the Senior Air Staff Officer at 10 Group
headquarters telephoned and told me he was preparing to fly
to Perranporth to see me. In due course a strange Spitfire
landed, taxied in, and I drove out to greet the pilot, who was
SASO 10 Group.

'I want to have a Top Secret discussion with you,' he said.

'Sure, sir. I'll drive you to my office.'

We entered, I sat him down and called for coffee which
tasted as if it were made of acorns.

He pulled a map from his briefcase, laid it on my desk. It
was a detailed ordnance map, and on it was drawn a red
ring.

'Recognize that?' he asked.

'Yes. It's part of the Brest Peninsula.' I looked more closely.
I jabbed my fingers on the map. 'That's the town of Lannion,
about ten miles from the ringed target.'

'Correct,' he replied. 'What do you think the target I have ringed is?'

'I haven't the faintest idea.'

'It's a terribly important target. It is a factory which distils industrial alcohol.'

He gazed at me to allow me to suck in the import.

'What is so important about that?' I inquired.

'Air Intelligence say the Germans are running short of industrial alcohol. I want you to obliterate that target. It might make the Germans sue for peace.'

I gazed at him blankly.

'They make enough gin in Holland to float a couple of battleships,' I remarked mildly.

'Now don't go around thinking you know more about these things than Air Intelligence. They say it's essential to the war effort that you obliterate that target.'

'Why me? All I've got is a dozen combat-ready Spitfires with 0.303-inch ammunition. I haven't got any bombs. All I could do would be to bust a few copper pipes in the plant, and the Germans would repair them in half an hour!'

'Look, Allen,' he mouthed. 'Don't you realize that a few incendiary bullets might set the installation alight and burn it to the ground?'

'No,' I replied. 'And how am I supposed to find the plant? I'd have to fly at sea level on a compass course, I wouldn't know how the winds varied over a hundred miles there and another hundred back, and from the air that installation would look about as big as a flea on a bear's back.'

'Orders are orders,' he bawled. 'Take off at dawn tomorrow and destroy that distillery.'

I strapped him into his Spitfire and off he went in a cloud of dust.

Then I called my flight commanders in.

'Change the ammunition loads in your aircraft pronto,' I said. 'I want fifty per cent armour-piercing and fifty per cent incendiary bullets loaded into the ammunition bays. Both of you select your six best pilots, which with me will make thirteen, one as a spare in case of an aircraft failing to start. Tell the ground crews to make sure all fuel tanks are full, and that the squadron will be taking off at dawn tomorrow. I've checked the weather and it will be OK.'

'What's the form?' George asked.

'Can't tell you. I'll brief the selected pilots here after dusk. I can tell you it's to do with gin fizz.'

They gazed at me like I'd gone bonkers and shambled off to organize things. I called in Beau.

'Get hold of that plan of Lannion airfield, Beau,' I said. 'And then come back and help me draw lines on a map.'

'Certainly,' Beau replied, speaking like a clergyman at a funeral.

I rang up the Met. forecasters and asked them for their forecasts for winds over the Atlantic next morning without specifying the Brest Peninsula – not an unusual request. The winds would be light and steady and I would need to fly about five degrees off true course to get to the target. I let Beau into the plot, knowing he would keep his mouth shut, and we examined the aerial reconnaissance photograph with care. There were no heavy flak guns in the area, not that they would have done us any harm at the height and speed we would be flying, but the airfield was heavily defended with light flak emplacements.

'It's going to be tough,' Beau remarked, in a voice as sepulchral as a priest in his confessional box. 'The German observer corps fire red Very cartridges when they see enemy aircraft approaching. Their colleagues to the rear do likewise when they see the red cartridges explode, even before they attempt to transmit their reports to their operations room. The gunners will be waiting for you.'

'They won't, you know, Beau,' I replied. 'Because I'm attacking from the south; through the back door, so to speak. They'll be expecting a direct attack from the north. We'll get them off balance.'

'Not a bad idea,' Beau said mournfully. 'But it's going to be somewhat dicey, even so.'

'Better than making a futile attempt to strafe a bloody gin distillery,' I suggested.

'True, true. The normal complement at Lannion consists of twenty to thirty Junkers 88s.'

At dusk I told the selected pilots of the plan to strafe Lannion airfield. They were to keep silent about the plan; they might even have to apply gags over their mouths if they tended to talk in their sleep. Any leak to a possible German agent might mean that we would be met by a wing of Messerschmitts, and they would be in an excellent position to shoot us all down. I explained that my essential difficulty relied on navigation. It was vital that we made landfall over a part of the Brest Peninsula which I could recognize from my studies of the maps. Having arrived over an identifiable pin-point, then I would have to map-read, as well as leading the squadron at tree-top height, which wasn't going to be easy. I wanted to pass low, three miles to the west of the airfield, track along for a couple of miles, and then make a steep climbing turn to about 700 feet, open my throttle to Buster, and run in on a straight course directly from the south. As we commenced our attack, each pilot was to select his personal target; but as another pilot might have chosen the same target, every man had to have his wits about him to avoid mid-air collisions. If this occurred, the evading pilot need not attempt to fire his guns; his job was to avoid a collision. I did not want a single Spitfire lost; but I did want as many Junkers 88s as possible destroyed. R/T silence was to be strictly observed during the long flight over the Atlantic, but pilots could transmit essential messages when we were over French soil, especially to assist my navigation. The relief pilot was to peel off and return to base when we were halfway to Brest assuming the other twelve Spitfires appeared to be serviceable.

Beau then gave the pilots a rundown of Lannion airfield, with details as to where the bombers were normally dispersed on the ground, where the flak emplacements were situated.

Then we all went to bed.

*

My Merlin throatily started at dawn the next morning, and twelve other pilots pressed their starting buttons when they saw my propeller turning. We taxied out, lined up in pairs on the runway, with the spare pilot on his own behind the squadron. We took off and immediately went into battle formation, nice and loose, and I gained height to 100 feet and stayed at that level. We passed over the coast at a selected point east of the Lizard, and I set course for the target, attempting to maintain course within an accuracy of half a degree, confirming the accuracy of my gyro-compass with the magnetic compass every five minutes. In due course, the spare pilot drew ahead of the squadron, waggled his wings and turned for base – lucky devil. At which point I began to suffer from 'enginitis'. This is a strange phenomenon which every experienced fighter pilot knows about. There you are, a hundred miles over the grey relentless Atlantic, entirely reliant on two banks of cylinders which depend on twelve sparking-plugs. At which point the gremlins come into their own. Let me explain:

> When you're seven miles up in the heavens
> And that's a hell of a lonely spot,
> And it's 50 degrees below zero,
> Which isn't exactly hot,
> When you're frozen blue like your Spitfire,
> And you're scared a Mosquito pink,
> When you're thousands of miles from nowhere,
> And there's nothing below but the drink –
> It's then you will see the gremlins,
> Green and gamboge and gold,
> Male and female and neuter,
> Gremlins both young and old.
> White ones'll wiggle your wing-tips,
> Male ones will muddle your maps,
> Green ones will guzzle your glycol,
> Females will flutter your flaps,
> Pink ones will perch on your perspex,

And dance pirouettes on your prop.
There's one spherical middle-aged gremlin
Who spins on your stick like a top . . .

It was quite true; pilots do get hallucinations when flying into
danger, enemy coast ahead. I suffered such hallucinations on
innumerable occasions, and I put them down to the gremlins,
part of the family of poltergeists. My engine would shudder,
my oil pressure gauge would suddenly slide to a dangerously
low level, my glycol temperature would suddenly climb beyond
the bounds of prudence, and my oxygen supply would show
empty. It doesn't matter whether you are flying at 40,000 feet
or at sea level. It happens, that's for sure. However, I told my
gremlins to go to the devil and pursued my course for the Brest
Peninsula with the squadron spread out alongside – each
pilot, no doubt, suffering form hallucinations similar to my
own.

Dead ahead there suddenly materialized the red cliffs of the
Peninsula, and I struggled to pull my maps from my flying
boots where I had put them. Yes! By some miracle the
promontory was the one I was searching for. There was even a
black and white lighthouse off-shore to confirm my point of
landfall. When we were half a mile from the cliffs, I broke R/T
silence.

'Climbing up to ground level. Turn your firing buttons on
to FIRE. No R/T chatter, but let me know if you see an
important pinpoint. Switch your gun-sights on to BRILLIANT.'

We hauled back on our control columns and just missed
the steep cliffs. I maintained my altitude over the land at 100
feet. Red Very lights began to explode among us as the
German observer corps recognized us as hostiles. As we
swept over France, further red Very cartridges exploded at
their zenith. I recognized a village which was one of my pin-
points, adjusted course by a few degrees, and swept along at
tree-top level. In about ten agonizing minutes, I saw
Lannion airfield about three miles to port. Lady Luck was
on my side. I flew on for a couple of miles and transmitted:

'Making steep climbing turn to port onto reciprocal heading. Levelling out at 700 feet. Will commence dive, throttling Buster, when airfield dead ahead. Flight leaders form line abreast, aircraft line abreast. Loose formation for attack. Pilots select individual targets. Watch out for mid-air collisions. Skid on approach to confuse flak. Out.'

I dived at the airfield as we came within range. The whole squadron was widely spread out in line-abreast formation on me. We covered the total breadth of the airfield. I bust the emergency seal on my throttle at the appropriate moment, and my Spitfire shuddered as the boost made her accelerate. I saw a Junkers 88 with mechanics working on it; alongside was a flak emplacement and the gunners' tracer zoomed over my head. I gave the gunners a burst which silenced the guns, and skidded to aim at the Junkers. It exploded, and I saw mechanics fly into the air simultaneously; some of them were in flames as their overalls caught fire. I glanced sideways, and took note of at least eight Junkers enveloped in flames.

'Skid like hell and get down to ground level,' I transmitted over the R/T.

We slid over the cliffs like bats out of hell. Then I saw a Junkers 88 flying on a steady course about 2,000 feet above us.

'Climbing to attack enemy aircraft above,' I transmitted. 'I will make only one passing attack. Take a pot-shot if you can, but it is at an impossible angle. Do not, repeat not, attempt more than one attack.'

I gave the Spitfire emergency boost once again, climbed vertically towards the Junkers 88, laid off as much deflection in my gun-sights as possible, and pressed the firing button. The guns ran out of ammunition before I could really close range. I saw no strikes on the Junkers. It was an unlikely shot under the circumstances, but I bet it put the wind up the crew.

'Disengage,' I transmitted. 'I am waggling my wings. Form up with me. We are returning to base – but we won't get there. We haven't enough fuel. Throttling back to conserve fuel.'

The squadron formed up on me and we idled our way to Cornwall. My eyes were concentrated fully on my fuel gauges and, second in priority, on my compasses. I headed for the Lizard, spotted Predannack airfield and we made a hasty landing. The last man in had two gallons of petrol in his tanks. The people at Predannack had no idea why we landed there, or what we had been up to. I lied and said we had performed a practice sweep in the vague direction of Brest, that I managed to lose myself, and that I wanted only twenty gallons of petrol per aircraft to enable us to fly back to Perranporth. They didn't believe me, of course, because the canvas covering every gun-port on every Spitfire had been blown away by our bullets.

We sidled back to Perranporth in staid fashion, and as I disembarked Beau met me.

'Group want to know whether you blew up the industrial alcohol distillery near Lannion,' he said.

'Let me get my breath back, Beau,' I told him. 'Then bring your forms along to my office and I'll give you a combat report. Just for starters, you can signal Group Headquarters that none of our pilots is missing. Also tell them that I will personally act as courier and bring my combat report to Box, just in case there is any problem of a technical nature which might need sorting out.'

Beau gave a wan smile like Charles I did when they placed his head on the chopping-block.

'In the first place they won't see the problem,' he explained with gallows humour. 'In the next place, they won't have the faintest idea of the solution. You, sir, have created your own dung-hill. Do not attempt to fly away from it; bury yourself so deep in it that no one will be able to dig you out. You, sir, have made a totally unauthorized attack on an important German air base. You won't half get it in the neck.'

'Get the chaps in here and we'll debrief them together,' I said.

Beau wandered away, shuffling like a monk in his cloisters.

We had a small squadron briefing-room, and by the time Beau had summoned the pilots, I had pinned on the board a map showing the extent of the Atlantic between Cornwall and Brest with my navigational lines drawn across the sea. I also had the aerial reconnaissance photograph of the airfield, and ordnance scale maps of Lannion and its environs pinned to the board.

'Better take notes, Beau,' I said. 'Assemble all the evidence, and then type out a comprehensive combat report which each pilot in the formation will countersign after I affix my signature.

'This is my report,' I said to Beau. I proceeded to dictate a few notes . . . 'I headed directly for the important distillery but it appeared to have vanished. It occurred to me that German intelligence had become aware of plans long laid for a fighter squadron to bring it toppling down from its edifice. Further to which, the weather was deteriorating with appalling rapidity, and fog was encroaching over the target area.'

'Visibility was about twenty miles, clear as my sister's eyes,' came a murmur.

'Don't put that remark in your report, Beau,' I said. 'It might spoil the effect.'

'I'm quite sure it would,' Beau replied dryly . . .

'I suppose you know that his first salvo missed you by inches?' my Number Two interposed.

After I had dictated my 'report', the pilots all explained in detail how they fared. Every pilot had given a long burst at his target. Some reported that his particular Ju-88 had exploded, others that his had collapsed onto its belly. Some had had the opportunity to fire at more than one Junkers. Beau totted up the figures.

'It seems that the squadron totally destroyed eight Junkers 88, and destroyed or seriously damaged another four. I would judge that possibly a further six were damaged, either badly or merely holed. I shall make out my report accordingly.'

'Tell Group,' I said, 'that I recommend that we be re-deployed to Warmwell in Dorset. From there we could strafe a number of German airfields on the Cherbourg Peninsula which are in easy range.'

I believe that No. 66 Squadron's strafing attack on Lannion was the first air strike in squadron strength in the Second World War. It was highly successful. Prisoner-of-war reports from German aircrew shot down within a fortnight after the attack confirmed that twelve Junkers 88 had been destroyed and others damaged. A number of ground crews were killed and certain vital installations damaged. We lost no aircraft.

14

Daily Routine

I rang up Athol Forbes at 10 Group HQ the next morning and told him I was driving to 10 Group Headquarters to hand in my combat report.

'What the hell have you been up to?' he inquired.

'Parachuting some cases of gin onto the Germans,' I explained.

'Sounds like you are in the soup. I'll lay on a room for you and a bevy of dancing girls. Stay a night here.'

'OK by me,' I replied.

I drove to Box with Beau's combat report hidden under the carpet of the car.

'Take a pew,' the Senior Air Staff Officer said. 'Did you blow up that industrial alcohol plant.'

'No, sir. It was a stupid target. And what's more you know it was.'

'Of course it was a stupid target, but I was under orders and I put you under orders to attack it. Do you mean you disobeyed orders?'

'Not really. I couldn't find the target so I attacked an opportunity target as we turned for home.'

He gazed at me suspiciously.

'What,' he inquired, 'was your "opportunity" target?'

'Lannion airfield,' I said.

'Lannion airfield! Why, that's the most important German bomber base on the Brest Peninsula! I've been trying to get Bomber Command to attack it for months!'

'Bomber Command couldn't hit a chicken with a shotgun at two yards,' I replied. 'Like to read my combat report?'

He put his long legs on his desk and read the report.

'Bloody good show,' he said. 'But you're in trouble. Air Intelligence sold the notion of strafing the distillery to the

AOC. He thought it would win the war.'

'Well, it wouldn't have had the slightest effect on the war. Nor will knocking off a dozen Junkers have much effect, except it put the wind up them and they will strengthen their defences. But better to destroy a dozen Junkers on one strafing attack instead of flying a couple of hundred sorties on interception courses and probably bagging none.'

'Good logic, old boy. But how am I going to get you out of trouble?'

'No need, sir. The target area proper was enveloped in fog. You can't fart against thunder, and you can't find a precise target in fog.'

'How foggy was it?' he asked with a gleam in his eye.

'Very bad. I had only about twenty miles visibility.'

He slapped his thigh, a habit of his, and roared with laughter.

'Right. Your report states that the target area was covered in fog. I suppose all your pilots will back up that statement?'

'Of course, sir. They were there, weren't they?'

'Good enough. I'll sell that to the AOC.'

'Thanks,' I replied.

'OK. Well, come along to the bar and have a drink to success.'

'That, sir, would give me great pleasure.'

Athol was standing at the bar, of course, surrounded by a positive harem of attractive WAAF officers.

'I've got a party laid on for you tonight,' he told me.

'Good show, sir. That'll suit me fine,' I replied.

'What's he been up to?' Athol asked the Senior Air Staff Officer.

'Nothing much. He made the usual sort of balls-up that we have come to expect. I'll tell you about it later.'

'Incidentally,' SASO said to me, 'call on me about 1500 hours after lunch. I've got something to talk to you about.'

I went to his office after lunch. He took me to the secret Intelligence briefing-room in the Operations Room. On the board was a map of the dreaded area of Brest, with aerial reconnaissance photographs showing the anchorage of three German capital-ships in Brest Harbour – *Scharnhorst*, *Gneisenau* and *Prinz Eugen*. They had created havoc in the Atlantic and managed to slip into Brest. Bomber Command had been hurling bombs at them by night for far too long without causing sufficient damage; the shipwrights repaired them easily, and they were set to steam out of Brest and make a run for the Baltic, which they did achieve in due course.

SASO walked up and down with his kind of one-legged gait, slapping his thigh sporadically.

'In a couple of weeks,' he said, 'Bomber Command is going to launch possibly the biggest daylight raid in history – about eighty aircraft, to send these ships to the bottom. The spearhead will be three American Flying-Fortresses attacking at an altitude of over 30,000 feet, manned by British aircrew. We have only three long-range Spitfire squadrons to act as fighter escort, one of which is yours. You are to lead the escorting wing of Spitfires.'

I walked across to the aerial photograph of Brest and the surrounding area and gave it a close inspection.

'Have you taken note of the heavy flak emplacements covering Brest?' I inquired.

'Hardly our job, old boy,' he replied. 'This is Bomber Command's plan. Your fighters are not to enter the flak zone, for your role is purely anti-fighter support. German fighters won't enter the flak zone, but they will try to pick off the bombers before they enter the flak zone and when they get the hell out. Your job will be to see to the fighters, nothing else. What do you think?'

'Well, we should have enough fuel as we will enter the target area at the same speed as the bombers. As you say, we should certainly not penetrate the flak for that would be pointless. But, of course, the Messerschmitts are armed with 20-mm cannon apiece, also heavy-calibre machine-guns, whereas our armament is comprised of nothing but 0.303-inch machine-guns. We'll be in difficulties. Furthermore, for all I know, the Luftwaffe has deployed Focke-Wulf 190s in the area, which would really catch us with our trousers down. Additionally, as the bombers will have to climb to 10,000 feet and above for their attack, German radars will have fifty miles' and more warning of our approach. Finally, Brest is the most heavily defended target in the world, and Bomber Command can't bomb precision targets with the slightest accuracy. In short the whole plan reminds me of my Aunt Fanny's cat. I suggest twenty-five per cent of our bombers will be shot down by flak, and no direct hit will be scored on any of the three ships. That's all I've got to say.'

'And Tiresias and Phineus, prophets old,' he quoth. 'But what the hell can I do about it? Bomber Command, the Admiralty, the War Cabinet – even the Prime Minister – insist that this is the most important raid ever planned.'

'Oh well, ours not to reason why, I suppose,' I said. 'I'll lead the Spitfire wing if you want me to.'

'You've got to lead the Spitfire wing, old boy,' he muttered. 'You will get secret instructions in due course. And bloody good luck.'

That evening, Athol laid on a party in his own inimitable style. He selected four gorgeous WAAF officers, three of whom looked willing, but the fourth was merely attractive save for the fact that her brow was slightly wrinkled, which might have meant that she was a deep thinker or, even worse, an intellectual. We partook of about sixteen cocktails at the bar in the officers' mess, and then piled into Athol's large RAF brake, and headed at high speed to Athol's favourite hostelry near the Pump Room in Bath. We didn't exactly sip the Spa waters, but tended to taste the quality of the champagne until closing time hove to. On the way back, I had formed a deep attachment to Jean, the little intellectual number, and made frequent attempts to remove her brassiere without her knowledge, while she kept on droning about Goethe's *Die Leiden des jungen Werthers*, and telling me she had not long been down from Girton. We returned to the bar at Box, and in due course I noted that Athol and three of the lovely WAAFs had vanished.

'My God,' I said out loud, 'he can't be doing all three at the same time!'

'No, my dear,' Jean mumbled. 'Goethe was very single-minded. Shall we away to my quarters and continue our discussion?'

I followed her to her room, whereupon she stripped off her skirt and lay on her iron bed, gazing at me coyly.

'You know,' she said demurely, 'I believe that I am too small to be successfully penetrated.'

'What a shame,' I muttered, but this time finding Goethe distinctly the more interesting of the two topics. 'Don't you find that Goethe's *Faust* formed a worthy close to the life of Germany's greatest man of letters. Surely you would agree that his . . .' and so saying I got onto a chair and jumped out of her window. I landed in a bog of sorts, rushed into the dark and managed to find my car. I drove more or less in a straight line back to Perranporth, and arrived as dawn was breaking.

At about this time, a vacancy arose for the appointment of Squadron Engineer Officer. A young man, about my age, turned up for interview looking very blue in his brand-new uniform. I asked him to sit down, and questioned him on his experience of aircraft engineering. He had studied mechanical engineering at a red-brick university, and the RAF had given him several courses on airframes, aircraft engines, undercarriage systems and so on.

'Can you patch up a bullet-hole in a fuselage with a bit of duralumin and rivet it in position?' I inquired.

'Well, no, sir. But surely I would have airmen under my command to do that sort of thing.'

'Maybe, maybe not. But you would have to be in a position to check that the work was done properly. And you wouldn't be in a position to declare the aircraft operational unless you yourself were capable of performing the task on your own.'

'I suppose I could learn,' he replied hesitatingly.

'I doubt if you would learn quick enough for my liking,' I said.

I then hurled him a barrage of questions. What was the most common reason for a Merlin engine to show oil pressure too low for safety? Why is it that the glycol temperature occasionally stayed constant, too high for safety? What inspections were necessary on aircraft tyres before take-off and on landing? What causes a sticky oleo-leg which makes the undercarriage slow in retracting? I grilled him for ten minutes and his normal reply was that he had not been taught such details on his courses, but no doubt he would learn. He was not a bad chap but he was useless to me. He couldn't give my hardened senior NCOs and other ranks any form of leadership whatsoever.

Finally I said, 'What's the standard practice in the Indian Army?'

'No one told me about Army practices.'

'Well, I'll tell you, and remember it to your dying day, while you're in the RAF or if, after the war, you decide to run your own garage. First feed your horses when you get back from patrol. Next, ensure that the needs of your soldiers are fully looked after. Last, think about your own comfort and convenience. Sorry. I can't accept you. Report back to Group. I'll tell them to give you a job at a Maintenance Unit, where you will have experienced engineering officers supervising you. You're not ready to run the engineering side of a fighter squadron. Have some lunch in the mess, and then drive back to Group.'

Then I immediately rang up the engineer officer at Group responsible for such appointments.

'Bert,' I said, 'that flying officer is no good to me. Stick him in a Maintenance Unit and give him more experience under officer supervision.'

George laughed down the telephone.

'I thought you'd say that! Still it was worth a try-on. So what do I do now?'

'Promote my Flight-Sergeant Kelly to warrant-officer rank, and make him my Squadron Engineer Officer.'

'They've got to hold commissioned rank,' he protested.

'No, they don't. A warrant officer is allowable on the establishment to be appointed Squadron Engineer Officer. Check it out.'

He fumbled through some documents, I could hear him over the telephone.

'You're right,' he grumbled.

'OK. I'll tell Kelly to sew a crown on his sleeves. You fix the paperwork.'

'No use farting against thunder, is there?' he moaned. 'All right, I'll date his promotion to warrant officer with effect from today.'

'Thanks, George. And don't send me university graduates who don't know the difference between a spanner and a pair of tits again.'

My French flight commander, Capitaine Claisse, was posted at about this time for Intelligence duties with the Free French, which brought up the problem of finding a new flight commander. I wanted one of No. 66 Squadron's pilots for the job; I didn't like officers strange to the squadron to be allowed to join our club. The obvious selection was Laddie Lucas, but the trouble was he had not yet managed to get in all that much combat experience. So I decided to practise the art of conmanship and went to see Jack Boret at Sector Headquarters .

I always found Jack affable and amiable, but he could be tough when the occasion demanded. He asked me to sit down and wondered what I wanted, but I wasn't going to come to the point at that early stage. I gave him details not revealed in the combat report on the Lannion raid.

We went on to talk about the aircraft utilization rate in the squadron which was as high as it could be without having every one of our aircraft being given major inspections with none on the front line. He congratulated me on sharply decreasing the flying accident rate on the squadron, which previously had been too high – due mainly to the unusual weather conditions in which we had to operate. He rang for coffee, stuck his jaw out and said: 'Apart from all this drawing-room conversation, what is it you are after?' What have you got up your satanic sleeve?'

I withdrew a green, confidential file from my briefcase and pushed it across the desk to Jack Boret, who quickly scanned it. Then he gazed at me over his hawk nose.

'Your latest confidential report on Pilot Officer P. B. Lucas?' he inquired.

'No, sir. My strong recommendation that you should approve of my selection which is that Laddie Lucas should be given field promotion to become my junior flight commander.'

Jack perused the lists showing the flying hours Laddie had acquired, and then read my personal appreciation of him as an officer, and as a fighter pilot.

'You've certainly given him a glowing write-up,' he remarked. 'But for God's sake, Dizzy, he hasn't done as many operational flying as the hours he spent in his pram as a baby. You can't be seriously putting him forward as a flight commander.'

'I am certainly most serious, sir,' I told him. 'He is a natural leader, he learns quickly, his eye for a ball-game is unsurpassed – which automatically makes him a potential fighter leader. The metabolism in both activities is synonymous as you should know. In any case, I want to groom him ahead of the moment for a big show. I am not prepared to accept an experienced fighter pilot from another squadron as my flight commander. We work as a team, and Laddie Lucas is part of my team.'

'I know of a very experienced pilot going spare,' Boret said. 'I'm inclined to ask for him to fill your vacancy for a flight commander.'

'If you did, sir,' I replied pompously, 'I would have to reconsider my position.'

'Meaning you would resign your command of No. 66 Squadron?'

'Exactly right, sir.'

Whereupon Jack Boret lay back in his chair and giggled until foam came out of his mouth. He wiped his eyes, put his feet on his desk, and gave me a lecture.

'You know, of course, that the new policy is to send fighter squadron commanders off on a rest from operations when they have clocked up 400 operational flying hours. How many operational hours have you flown?'

I had flown 300 hours on combat missions, and a couple of hundred sorties over convoys. By my reckoning they couldn't kick me out until I'd put in about another 500 combat sorties.

Jack Boret began to wipe the tears from his eyes once again.

'Dizzy,' he said soothingly, 'I know exactly what figures you write in your flying log-book. After all, I do have to countersign it every month. I know you've been fiddling the books to remain with No. 66 Squadron. You, my dear chap, are living on borrowed time. Now don't go away with the impression that I will inform Group of what I know to be true. But they will catch you out sooner or later, mark my words.'

'OK, sir,' I replied. 'Thanks for keeping mum about it. But I still want Laddie Lucas as my junior flight commander. I want him more especially for the big show.'

'All right. I will endorse your recommendation for his promotion to acting flight lieutenant. But you realize, of course, it is most irregular to promote a pilot officer to the rank of acting flight lieutenant. Normally, only flying officers can be given such a jump in the promotion stakes.'

'For your information, sir,' I said, 'I am a substantive flying officer cum acting flight lieutenant, cum acting squadron leader. If you kicked me out, I would revert to the rank of flying officer and would come under the flying leadership of someone or other who wouldn't know what he was doing, in my considered view. But I know very well what I am doing in the case of Laddie Lucas. He may not be an exceptional pilot at this stage, but he is an exceptional officer and leader.'

'There won't be any argument,' Jack Boret said. 'Here: I am endorsing your report requesting that Pilot Officer Lucas is to be given the acting rank of flight lieutenant, and to be appointed in command of B Flight, No. 66 Squadron. I will forward it to Group through my channels. Tell him to put up his badges of rank tomorrow.'

'Thanks very much,' I replied. 'I had no doubt that you would support me on this.'

'So I have. Now what's this "big show" you keep talking about?'

Whereupon I gave Jack Boret the general rundown on the proposed raid on Brest in daylight by Bomber Command, also our role in acting as escorts. I told him the plan stank like the devil always leaves a stink behind him, that the planners should be immediately placed in close confinement in Bedlam or shot dead or given hefty doses of cyanide.

He looked at me gloomily.

'It's bloody lunacy,' he sighed. 'But do realize that Bomber Command are being pressurized by the Admiralty, the Chiefs of Staff Committee; and that, no doubt, Winston Churchill thinks it a hell of a good show. So don't blame them. When's it coming off?'

'Within a week or so. No doubt they will have the decency to inform you in good enough time. All the escort fighters will have to deploy into the stations contained in your sector ahead of the operation. We'll have only three Spitfire squadrons, and I've been told to lead the wing. Better get your air-sea rescue services tuned up. You will be needing them.'

I rose, saluted and left leaving Jack Boret rubbing his nose thoughtfully.

15

Necessary Chores

Top Secret signals began to flow in outlining the plan – some plan – to bomb the three German capital-ships lying in Brest harbour. Two 'long-range' Spitfire squadrons would deploy to Portreath, and we would deploy south to Predannack airfield to get maximum radius of action from that forward base. I arranged with the other two fighter squadron commanders to fly at the same height as the main force of the bombers, and we would fly 8,000 feet above to act as top cover to get the jump on the Messerschmitts diving at the bombers.

The three Flying-Fortresses could fly at 35,000 feet, but the British aircrew had little experience in flying these aircraft, and these B-17s were not modified to full American standards. I am pretty sure that they were not equipped with the top-secret Norden bomb-sight, gyroscopically controlled, which could indeed 'drop a bomb into an apple-barrel from 35,000 feet'. By comparison, British bomb-sights in those days might have been invented by Heath Robinson. It would take a very lucky bomb to damage these battle-cruisers, which carried armour plate designed to withstand the forces of 15-inch shells. In fact, the total concept of the operation was a farce, and an extremely dangerous farce at that.

At H-hour we scrambled from Predannack and climbed to intercept the main stream of bombers – there was no need for fighter protection for the Flying-Fortresses which could fly so high to make it not worthwhile for German fighters to climb to that altitude, especially as they had so many juicy targets flying at medium height. I saw the other two Spitfire squadrons form up as close escort to the bombers and climbed another 8,000 feet to maintain top cover. British

bombers could not fly in close formation, for as they
operated normally at night that would have been pointless.
They flew in a cumbersome stream, which meant that the
gunners in one bomber could not give much support to their
colleagues in another. (The Americans always flew in close
formation in their daylight attacks, and as each B-17 carried
about eleven gunners armed with the formidable Point-Five
machine-gun, as the gunners in one aircraft could give heavy
and concentrated fire support to their colleagues in the
formation, they presented formidable targets for the
Luftwaffe. The Germans eventually conquered this problem
by the use of head-on attacks, and then by firing rockets well
out of range of the gunners.)

Furthermore, since the bombers were flying in an
ungainly stream some ten miles in length, spread over
thousands of acres of airspace, it was literally impossible to
provide effective fighter escort, especially with only three
Spitfire squadrons. If there had been 300 British fighter
squadrons, even that would have made no sense, because the
all-important German defences relied on flak, more efficient
and far greater in effectiveness than the whole of the London
anti-aircraft barrage combined. No doubt the bomber crews
well appreciated that they were being cast into hell and that
the odds were loaded against them, but they flew on to their
destiny with great steadfastness. R/T silence was observed
and that was a farrago, for no one could call the stragglers to
heel, and in any case German radars had sighted the force
not long after it crossed the Cornish coast. Reinforcing
Messerschmitts were flying into the airfields around Brest by
then, and all the ammunition required was being stacked by
the heavy flak guns.

The moment we crossed the coast of the Brest Peninsula,
the forward flak guns began ranging fire on the bombers. We
stayed above for the guns would be aiming at the bombers
and would not bother with a mere squadron of fighters, but
the other two Spitfire squadrons opened out wide from the
bomber stream, acting in a strictly anti-fighter role as

briefed. As the bomber stream closed on the target, I noted that the capital-ships were engulfed in a smokescreen – not unnaturally. I also took note of a positive barrage of flak shells bursting amidst the bomber stream. Black it stood as night, fierce as ten furies, terrible as hell. At one moment in time I saw five blazing bombers spinning down to their doom, and I felt sick. The bombing was not concentrated, of course, and probably did little more than destroy a few fishermen's cottages on the outskirts of Brest. There were so many parachutes in the air I couldn't count them. It was bloody murder, planned and conceived by raving lunatics.

Many of the bombers turned for base before reaching the central target area, and I didn't blame them, they might have been damaged. Should I turn with them and give them cover on their way out? No. I stayed with the hard core of bomber crews who pressed on to the target area proper. The other two Spitfire squadrons could look after those who had turned back. Those bombers which continued into the midst of this inferno made an ungainly wheel after dropping their bombs. As they flew away from the flak barrage, I watched out for Messerschmitts now free to come in and finish off the slaughter of these innocents. They came hurtling down, and we turned onto them, breaking up their formations. The air was thick with fighters, mostly German. A few dog-fights ensued and I fired my guns on two occasions. We then escorted the bombers under our protection over the sea, outside the range of the Me-109s.

As the bombers crossed the Cornish coast, I flew close to the leading bomber aircraft, waggled my wings and dived for Predannack with the squadron behind me. I took note of a gaping hole in the fuselage of his aircraft. We landed at our forward base with all too little petrol in our tanks. I learned later that several bombers had crash-landed on English soil en route to their home bases; a number of aircrews were killed in these crashes.

The lunatic, the lover and the poet are of imagination all compact. There were no lovers or poets on the Air Staff.

* * *

Since we were short of German targets to shoot at, I
instigated a form of gunnery range out to seaward from
Perranporth. We fired at yellow buoys and the occasional
drogue being hauled by a drogue-towing aircraft. We
signalled the Admiralty to show the area on the charts as a
firing range, but the odd fishing-boat – probably not
carrying charts – tended to infringe the area. We only fired in
good visibility, so it was easy enough to stop firing as these
boats entered the out-of-bounds segment. Whereupon we
would fly and beat hell out of the offending skipper,
approaching at sea level and hauling up to just clear his
rigging. One over-enthusiastic pilot misjudged this manoeuvre and removed the mainmast. This made a large hole in
his wing, but we removed a wing from an old wreck and
patched it up. What the skipper thought about it I will never
know.

One day I was returning from firing at a drogue, when I
saw a large – by the standards of the day – bomber limping in
to land at Perranporth with smoke pouring from one of its
two engines.

'Jeez!' I thought. 'I must have shot at it!'

I formated on it, and the pilot gave me the thumbs-up
signal and grinned. It occurred to me that he was a very
forgiving man. I kept with him until he hit the runway on one
engine, the propeller of the damaged engine was feathered; I
did a circuit and landed after him.

'What happened?' I inquired as he scrambled from the
cockpit, while the fire-engine, directed foam onto the
burning engine. 'And what is this monstrosity you've been
flying?'

'I'm a test pilot from A. V. Roe,' he replied. 'And this
monstrosity is the Manchester.'

'But it's far too large for two engines,' I said. 'It would be
pretty effective with four engines though.'

'You can say that again,' he replied. 'Mind you, these
engines are extremely powerful. They are Rolls-Royce
Vultures and develop about 2,000 hp each.'

'Even so, a big twin-engine bomber like this is utterly vulnerable to enemy attack, whether by flak or German fighters.'

'You've given me an idea,' he replied 'I reckon that if we stretch the fuselage a bit, and strengthen the wing loading member, we could redesign this aircraft as a four-engine aircraft powered by Merlins.'

'Makes sense to me,' I said. 'Incidentally, I didn't put a bullet in your engine, did I? I've just been exercising my guns.'

'No. The engine failed over Newquay, miles away from here. It's the third Vulture which failed while I was flying a Manchester, which is not only tedious, but bloody dangerous.'

'Come and have a drink,' I said. 'We'll arrange to fly you and your crew back to your factory airfield.'

'I'll take the drink, and thanks. But I'll have to arrange with A. V. Roe to fly down a team of technicians, also a new engine, and get the bloody thing serviceable.'

Whenever I think of the Air Staff, a verse of Edward Lear's springs to mind: 'There was an old man with a beard,/Who said, "It is just as I feared!/Two owls and a hen,/Four larks and a wren,/Have all built their nests in my beard." '

The Manchester was a sick joke, a heavy bomber powered by only two Vulture engines. No regard was paid to the vulnerability of a bomber of that size with two engines. The whole concept of the design, specified by the Air Ministry, was Alice in Wonderland.

However, A. V. Roe and Rolls-Royce took the Manchester to bits and redesigned it, replacing the two Vultures with four Merlin engines. And lo and behold, from their design and research departments there came the mighty Lancaster, the most successful night bomber of the war. It not only carried five-ton skip bombs on the dams raids; it also carried the Grand Slam which weighed no less than ten tons.

That the Air Ministry can do no wrong is a necessary and

fundamental principle of the English constitution. A sentiment with which I disagree.

Although flying was my true love, there was a certain amount of administrative work to be done when commanding a fighter squadron. My *eminence grise* was, of course, my Intelligence Officer, Beaufort-Palmer. His wife used to drive down, and he would either take a few days' leave on her arrival or spend his day working until I gave him the wink to leave his military duties and attend to those matrimonial. She always brought with her, as I remember, two large Samoyed, Arctic dogs, not dissimilar to Chows but with pointed faces and coloured white. Both she and Beau were gentle people, and how he put up with the stink of 100-octane petrol, the roar of the Merlins, the profanity of the language used by both pilots and ground crew, I simply do not know. Yet Beau seemed to enjoy his military service, although I had a sneaking feeling that he would have preferred to be checking up on his views of Sophocles. It was really a strange situation with Beau, a highly educated man, possibly a don pre-war, coming under the orders of someone who had just passed from his twenty-first year into his twenty-second. Whatever distaste Beau might have felt, to me he was my friend and mentor – a strange relationship indeed.

Pilots were killed now and again in flying accidents. One pilot would (inadvertently) chop the tail off the Spitfire of another, and so on. In such cases, I would have to convene things called Committees of Adjustment. I sat on several when I was a bog-rat at Lossiemouth, so I knew the procedures. Normally we used the padre as Head of the Committee of Adjustment at Lossiemouth or other stations, but at Perranporth we were not possessed of a station chaplain, so, more often than not, Beau would be detailed as President of the Committee. It was a melancholy task, sombre, sad, dispiriting. If the body hadn't fallen into the sea or been smashed into small pieces on contact with mother earth, the committee would need to see the post-mortem report. It was none of their business how the fatality occurred; their job was to sort out the personal effects of the dead man. I had to write letters of condolence to the next of kin.

For a start, the dead pilot's bedroom door would be locked and sealed, and the windows would also be sealed. In due course the committee would search through the late lamented's belongings. Valuable articles such as gold cuff-links, pocket watches, photographs of sentimental value and so on would be written on an inventory. His wallet would be searched, and his money, his cheque book, personal photographs, etc., would be scrutinized. His bank statements would be inspected, and insurance policies or share certificates. His letters would be read, so would photographs of his girlfriends or mistresses. Many's the letter I have torn into shreds; many's the photograph of a nude girl I have destroyed from a dead man's kit. One always had to balance possibilities. If the parents thought that their son walked in a virgin wilderness, who was I to disillusion them shortly after he had died on active service? It was the most nauseating of all the tasks I ever had to undertake, prying through the secrets of a dead man, no longer able to defend or excuse his secret life. But we parcelled up the clothing, put into the crate sealed envelopes marked 'personal and private' which we agreed the parents could keep as souvenirs. Then the crate would be dispatched on a lorry or in a van to the central authority responsible for the personal effects of officers and other ranks.

When fatal accidents occurred, Courts of Inquiry were inevitably established, unless the pilot was killed in action. If a member of my squadron was killed while flying non-operationally, as a number of them were, I was not appointed as president or member of the Court in case I was found blameworthy. I mean, if a squadron commander sends off a pilot on an exercise for which he is inadequately trained, then the squadron commander is culpable. But I had to sit on scores of courts of inquiry during my Air Force career, and I developed an incredible knack of discovering exactly how the pilot died. I cannot go into any detail for want of space. But I can say that, somehow, I managed to get inside the pilot's mind just before the moment of impact. I believe in ghosts, and I also believe in extra-sensory perception. My ghosts let me into their secrets. One impossible Court of Inquiry occurred in Germany in 1958, when a dual-controlled Meteor jet plunged into a block of flats. Most of the witnesses were German, and my interpreter had to make some sense out of their descriptions, most of which were totally inaccurate and totally useless. The 'instructor' was in the front seat and was killed on impact. The 'pupil' in the rear seat had a leg torn off. I gave him four days to recover in part before we went to see him. He remembered nothing whatsoever about the accident.

Six weeks later, I reconvened the Court, and we went to see the surviving pilot once more.

'Tell me what you remember about the crash,' I asked him.

He wrinkled his brow.

'Nothing,' he said eventually.

'OK. Now I'll tell you exactly what happened in my view.' And I did.

'No. I can't remember anything.'

We wrote out our conclusions and recommendations, and that was the end of that.

Six years later, the one-legged pilot contacted me.

'My memory has suddenly come back. Let me tell you exactly what happened when we crashed.'

'Go ahead,' I replied.

Word for word he told me in precise detail exactly what we had written in our findings, conclusions and recommendations.

Meanwhile, the Air Ministry Accident Prevention Branch had taken note of our findings. They wrote in their journal an article, discussing the ability of Sherlock Holmes, had he been in charge of the inquiry. They reckoned he couldn't have done it better than I and my colleagues had. They gave it the title 'The Spider's Web'. I was the spider-monkey hovering on the side-lines.

There were all sorts of details to keep under control, some of the utmost importance, others mundane. The orderly officer was supposed to look after the welfare and food of the airmen, but such aspects were to me of far too vital importance to leave to a pilot officer. Any and every senior NCO and airman was allowed free access to me if required. If he thought that his flight-sergeant or his flight commander had handed out an injustice, then I insisted that he should be brought along to see me – together with his superior whom he considered had been unfair. If he was a malingerer, as some were, he would receive rough justice from me, and his superior officer would get my full support on his judgment. The word got around, and the malingerers tended to accept the judgment of their immediate superiors, and not ask to see me. But there were a few men whose case or plea had been misunderstood. Did they or did they not deserve to be given compassionate leave because the wife was having a baby, or the father was dying from booze? I always had the particular airman's reports to hand, and I normally knew whether he was a good'un or a bad'un. Field punishment was still allowed in those days, and whereas we didn't tie the malingerers with rope to chariot wheels and whip the horses into a gallop, I could order a man to run round the airfield perimeter three times with a 60-lb pack on his back – and I occasionally did. The genuine cases were fairly obvious, especially when the Squadron Sergeant Major had given me the wink. They would be given free railway warrants and a fortnight's compassionate leave if one felt such treatment to be warranted.

Another, but important, chore was to write confidential reports on officers. This was not as important in war as in peace, because in war promotion came swiftly – all too swiftly on occasions – according to the number of aircraft

destroyed by a pilot. In the Battle of Britain, the norm was
that one should have destroyed six German aircraft before
being awarded the Distinguished Flying Cross. But these
were normally shot down over British soil, and it was not too
difficult to correlate claims for aircraft destroyed, by
reference to the claimant's combat report, the time of the
victory and the general area in which the enemy aircraft
should have crashed. Police and Royal Observer reports of
the whereabouts of crashed aircraft were also useful in this
context. I was denied claims of at least ten aircraft which
crashed into the sea. One Dornier collected a salvo of my
bullets, one engine was burning fiercely as it spun into the
cloud directly over London, and oil from the stricken engine
poured back like a whiplash and covered my windshield with
thick oil. I had to return to base by reference to my
instruments, and landed with my head stretched out of the
cockpit because I had no forward vision. Yet I was allowed
one Dornier damaged by our addle-minded Intelligence
Officer. Apart from a general sense of indignation, such
stupidity didn't affect me. One more Hun had bit the dust,
no matter how our imbecilic IO viewed the matter. Not that
he viewed the matter; he was crouching in an air-raid shelter
with a tin hat on his head!

But the assessment of officers for what they are worth and,
more important, how one views their potential in senior
rank, is something that should not be taken lightly. This does
not mean that you follow an officer around with a telescope
in the hand, nor do you lie under his bed taking note of his
sexual habits. It is axiomatic that a good officer should be a
good pilot in the General Duties Branch of the RAF. But
what one is seeking, that fairly simple diagnostic aspect
apart, is the quality of leadership; and as this is almost
impossible to define or explain, this makes the job no easier.
In such terms, I put my finger on Laddie Lucas and fiddled
him into the appointment as my flight commander. He went
on to do daring and dashing things in the defence of Malta,
transferred to Bomber Command flying Mosquitoes,

finished the war with a DSO and bar, and a DFC, went on to become a Member of Parliament for ten years, and was then promoted from Managing Director to Chairman of the Greyhound Racing Board – a big financial company indeed. But it wasn't too difficult to pick out the mature, *soigné*, well-mannered Laddie, who knew – the most important point of them all – how to handle his senior NCOs and airmen. I could quote scores of cases when I pushed the right chap in the right direction – upwards. Perhaps I generally tended to over-assess my officers, because as they were part of the various squadrons I commanded and, assuming they did their jobs to my satisfaction, they were members of the kindergarten over which I presided. But if I had to use the hatchet, then I had no compunction in wielding it.

Similarly with senior NCOs, most of them fine men. But were they made of commissionable material? A number of senior NCOs – for reasons of inverted snobbery or sheer funk – would have refused a commission if I had offered to recommend them to officer rank. That didn't mean they were not first-class NCOs. A bright, enthusiastic airman was always worth keeping an eye on. If his work was good or better, if he was prepared to service an aircraft in the snow and refuse to have his dinner in the cookhouse until he had finished the job, such a man was a good 'un.

The most difficult task for a squadron commander was to come to the firm conclusion that a pilot was suffering from 'lack of moral fibre' – i.e. fear of flying, fear of being engaged with the enemy, or both. The brain is the most complex organ of them all, and slight derangement can have fearful results – fear of the dark, fear of the world outside, fear of heights, fear of cats; even fear of women, although I must confess to have never suffered from that particular kind of phobia. A number of men simply did not know what they were taking on when they enthusiastically applied for flying training. Even at my elementary flying training school I took note of three pilots who were downright scared of flying. It is most difficult to pick out a man who is suffering from lack of moral fibre, which he may not have shown during his flying training, but which hits him right between the eyes when he joins an operational squadron and appreciates that he might be shot at.

Bomber operations differed widely in psychological stress from fighter operations. We became attuned to 'going over the top' five or six times a day, and since, in 1940, the odds were normally laid heavily against us, for the Luftwaffe could concentrate their raids outside our radius of action and then alter their course in mass formations towards England, the tensions we suffered wrecked our metabolism. Added to this was sheer physical exhaustion. Climbing to 30,000 feet and above several times a day, with irregular intakes of food, was intensely fatiguing. The physical effect this had on the human body has not yet been researched. Pure oxygen is not a good gas to breathe for five hours a day. Then again, the colon would expand quite slowly as one gained height, and contract very quickly as one dived either at the enemy or to escape his clutches. Anyone who ate peas with his meals would be practically blown out of his cockpit by the power of his farts.

Bomber operations had the advantage that there were five or more aircrew members in the same aircraft. The Germans recognized the importance of such camaraderie and designed their bombers in the main so that each crew member was in touching distance of another. But the shivering rear gunner in a Lancaster would be thirty feet away from his colleagues, desperately lonely; and he knew that, more likely than not, he would be the first to die. Bomber operations needed an ice-cold courage. For eight hours the aircraft would be over hostile territory, while the biggest firework display ever seen in world history would be emanating from the ground. And, of course, the flash of every flak gun impressed on the mind that the shell was aimed at you personally, not at any of the other 800 bombers surrounding you. Modern civil-airline pilots write indignant reports today about near-misses if another airliner comes to within two miles of them. Bomber Command's aircraft were only a few hundred yards away from one another, at night with no warning lights turned on. No one has established the number of mid-air collisions suffered by Bomber Command. The mathematicians calculated a two per cent risk. I believe that six per cent of British bombers collided with each other in the black of the night. But the point is that the aircrew were aware of these risks, even if the scientific analysts were not.

I had a doctor established with me in No. 66 Squadron, but he was of little use. In theory the diagnosis of LMF was the joint responsibility of the squadron commander and the squadron medical officer. I didn't even bother to consult him when I met a particularly newly joined pilot and immediately diagnosed that he was suffering from LMF, nor did I consult my flight commander to whose flight I appointed the suspect pilot. Sure as eggs are eggs, my flight commander saw me within a fortnight and told me that, in his view, this pilot was suffering from LMF. I wrote out the symptoms on a form marked 'Medical Confidential', showed it to the doctor who countersigned it, although he really hadn't the first idea of what it was all about. Then I gave it to the pilot to read and countersign, which he did. He was grounded, and in due course appeared before the psychiatrists who confirmed my opinion and removed him from flying duties.

On another occasion, we were deployed to Hampshire to take part in a sweep over France. There was a particular pilot attached to one of the other squadrons who was heavily decorated for his claims during the Battle of Britain. I met him for the first time and I didn't like what I saw. I told my senior flight commander that I would break formation as and when I thought necessary with my Number Two, and that he was to lead the squadron when I departed. He gazed at me blankly and nodded. As we flew over the Channel I kept a close eye on the squadron the pilot referred to was flying with, and sure enough I saw a Spitfire peel off and dive to sea level. My Number Two and I broke formation and followed at a discreet distance; whereas we just managed to keep him in sight, he would have had the utmost difficulty in spotting us. In due course, he made several turns over the empty sea, and I opened my throttle sufficiently to get to within about a mile of him. He fired his guns into the sea, kept turning circles, and then set course for base. We managed to intercept the wing and I took up the lead from my flight commander, and in due course we landed back at our forward base in Hampshire.

There was the usual debriefing after such a sweep, and no pilot claimed so much as having seen a German aircraft. However, the pilot I had been following claimed that he was jumped by Messerschmitts, broke formation and followed them down. He indulged in a ferocious dog-fight at sea level, and shot down four Messerschmitts. They all exploded as his bullets made impact. The assembled pilots gave a cheer. 'Good old . . .' they exclaimed. 'He's done it again.'

He had done it again, but once too often.

I asked to see the Sector Commander of the station we were deployed to. I took my Number Two with me. I reported to him in full the incident, the false claims of which we two were witnesses.

'Thanks a lot,' the Sector Commander said. 'I've had my doubts for some time. He will not be granted any of the claims he made on this sweep. He will be removed from the General Duties Branch, and given a commission in one of the ground branches.'

If you had no sense of dignity, honour, integrity – and human modesty – you could get away with murder in these terms. Alas, a number of pilots in Fighter Command did get away with this sort of criminality. But, I fear, I have researched the subject in depth, and I can tell the good'un from the bad'un at the drop of a hat.

Epilogue

No. 66 Squadron was formed at Filton near Bristol, in 1916. It was soon deployed to support the BEF in France, equipped with fighters, Sopwith Pups. It was in action during the Battle of Arras when it flew offensive patrols in support of the British Army, acted as bomber escort and indulged in aerial reconnaissance. It also acted in a fighter-bomber role, and operated in a strafing role during the Battle of Messines, attacking German infantry and transports. It was moved to the Calais region, acting as an interceptor fighter squadron against the daylight bomber raids on London in 1917. During the summer and autumn of 1917, the squadron was heavily engaged in the Battle of Ypres performing a variety of multi-combat tasks – attacking German observation balloons, bombing and strafing German-held airfields, striking at barges, motor transports and infantry as they attempted to reinforce their front lines.

In November 1917, No. 66 Squadron was re-deployed to the Italian front to assist the hard-pressed Italian armies. It re-equipped with the excellent Sopwith Camel, and gave the Austrian Army and Air Force a hard time. As the war drew to an end, it became famous as a hard-hitting ground attack squadron, destroying numbers of enemy aircraft on the ground and causing damage to airfields and industrial installations. During the last three weeks of the First World War, it was solely occupied in almost continuous bombing and strafing of the retreating Austrian armies.

No. 66 Squadron returned to England in 1919 and the squadron was thereupon disbanded. A member of the squadron, Lieutenant Jerrard, had been awarded the VC in March 1918.

Clickety-Click was re-formed at Duxford on 20 July 1936

when Fighter Command was established and equipped with the biplane Gloster Gauntlet fighter. It was the second fighter squadron in the RAF to be equipped with Spitfires, shortly before the war, No. 19 being the first, also stationed at Duxford, but these early Spitfires Mk I were hardly combat ready.

In 1929 the Air Staff offered aircraft manufacturers to tender for the design of 'an impossible fighter', capable of flying at 255 mph on the straight and armed with four machine-guns. In 1929 the Supermarine S5 float-plane had already won the Schneider Trophy lap at a speed of 328.63 mph. In 1931 the Supermarine S6B, powered by a 2,300 hp Rolls-Royce engine, finally won the Schneider Trophy at an average speed of 340.8 mph on the triangular course, meaning that it had to exceed 400 mph on the straight. The Air Staff were not impressed and insisted on going ahead with their 'miracle' fighter. Whereupon Vickers, a subsidiary company of which was Supermarine, arranged with Rolls-Royce to design their own fighter, adding the codicil that no technical member of the Air Staff would be allowed through the doors of their secret design offices or their factories. From this private venture came the Rolls-Royce Merlin, the most successful aero-engine of the war; and the highly engineered Spitfire, designed by R. J. Mitchell. The Air Staff didn't like it, and their abhorrence for it remained in situ after its first successful encounter over Dunkirk. The fact that it was highly engineered meant that it took longer to produce than the Hurricane, but if there had been any sanity within the Air Staff, these difficulties could have been ironed out.

The Hurricane was in a different class from the Spitfire; it was a hack, whereas the Spitfire was a racehorse. However, due to its sturdy construction, the Hurricane could accept heavy damage in combat, and it was also a good aircraft in field conditions, where it could operate well because of its sturdy, well spaced-out undercarriage. The designer was Sidney Camm, who modelled it on his successful Hawker Fury biplane, and it was powered by the same Merlin engine as the Spitfire. As it received more official support than the Spitfire, the production of Hurricanes was much greater initially. Consequently, in 1938 there were five squadrons of Hurricanes in service, but adjustments and modifications had to be made after spinning trials showed deficiencies, and the greases in the guns froze at height because the gun heating was inadequate. There were then only two Spitfires in squadron service on an experimental basis.

The pro-Hurricane school solemnly believe that their aircraft was on the same plane as the Messerschmitt 109, and they are widely wrong. They base this spurious conclusion on the fact that more German aircraft were shot down in 1940 by Hurricanes than by Spitfires. This is special pleading, although the statistics are accurate. As there were far more Hurricanes than Spitfires in action, and as there were, therefore, a greater number of 'aces' flying Hurricanes than Spitfires and, finally, since the front-line airfields in the Battle of Britain were occupied mainly by Hurricanes, it was natural that Hurricane pilots had more successes – and disasters – than Spitfire pilots. Against that, Douglas Bader's Big Wing, based on East Anglia, was mainly equipped with Hurricanes. He used three, or sometimes four, squadrons in his Big Wing, which in theory represented a condition of overwhelming air superiority wherever he decided to fly. The (sieved and sifted) claims made by the Big Wing could be described as somewhat exaggerated.

Clickety-Click was most certainly my Alma Mater, and my two senior professors were Rupert Leigh and Athol Forbes. In sheer terms of intellect I would give Rupert pride of place. But Athol had his qualities too – the murderous instinct which any fighter pilot must possess; the panache, the *élan*, the sheer sophistication of joy in combat. It is not only difficult, it is stupid, to attempt to compare two men in detail. It is sufficient to say that I was fortunate enough to sit on my bench while the two finest tutors I could have ever wished for explained what the chalk marks on the blackboard meant, when turned into white-hot combat. A further benefit was that, although they were trained murderers of Germans, they were both *gentle* men. They transmuted me from a lad to a man; they transmogrified me over the mountains of the moon. In humble duty I give them my sincere thanks and all expressions of gratitude.

After I was almost forcibly removed from my command of No. 66 Squadron in 1942, my replacement only lasted a couple of days before being killed in a mid-air collision. The squadron then moved to Portreath, and then to Warmwell, near Chesil Bank. At this point the outstanding fighter pilot, Squadron Leader Bob Yule, DFC, took command, and the squadron was mainly occupied in fighter sweeps over France. It specialized in attacks on shipping at ports like Cherbourg, and was equipped with cannon-firing Spitfires Mk V. Later, equipped with the superlative Spitfire Mk IXB, the squadron went to France acting in a fighter/ground attack role. After Fighter Command was virtually disbanded in the late 1950s, it was re-equipped with helicopters and based on Odiham in Hampshire. It was then sent to Singapore where it was disbanded in 1969. The No. 66 Squadron history was written by Squadron Leader Sammy Osborne, DFC, who was in command while it still held a fighter role. The history is contained in a leather-bound volume, complete with photographs, and resides in the archives of the Ministry of Defence.

By the time I left No. 66 it had made of me an experienced fighter pilot and fighter leader. But in truth, I didn't know the half of it. My nineteenth birthday had gone forever when I joined as a bog-rat, but my twenty-second birthday had not struck me when I assumed command of 66 Squadron. If this was my apprenticeship, which it was, I had to learn fast. My German tutors were also good at their job – there is nothing quite like a load of red-hot lead up the backside to remove one's conceit. I was wounded on four occasions, concussed twice, and bailed out once. But retribution came swiftly to my enemies when I began to appreciate that aerial combat does not equate with dancing in the dark.

'The brazen throat of war had ceased to roar,/All now was turned to jollity and game,/To luxury and riot, feast and dance.' John Milton must have had an as yet unobserved sense of humour. My brazen throat of war did not cease when the Second World War ended. It was as brazen as ever when I left my command of a wing of nuclear/strike, photo-reconnaissance, and night-fighter aircraft in 1965 after having been in the RAF for a generation of a man's life. We were always at the ready – even on Christmas Day – to oppose our enemies so far as our puny resources permitted. It takes, I believe, fifteen years for a novice in the Society of Jesus to become an accredited Jesuit. In my day, it took at least twenty years' apprenticeship for an aviator to be a fully accomplished military pilot. The ultimate was to manoeuvre the aircraft high in the azure skies, finish one's exercise and descend, when thick, black turbulent cloud enveloped one's aircraft at about 20,000 feet. From then on, with no outside orientation, you were utterly dependent on the flying instruments, no matter whether they all were in working order, or only some of them were. The heater on the pitot-head might have failed, leaving it iced up and unable to give any indication at all of your air speed, which was a vital factor. The artificial horizon might have gone wonky, but the attitude of the aircraft could be gauged by taking regard of the turn and slip indicator, the rate of descent and climb indicator, and so forth. Perhaps the undercarriage might fail to lock down on selection despite the emergency system, then the only recourse was to jettison the overload tanks on a safe part of the airfield, and belly-land on the grass. A hundred different emergencies might arise, and it was up to you, and you alone, to deal with the problems or die in the attempt. I would not like to calculate the number of pilots in my squadrons, or in other squadrons based on the same air-fields as myself, who were killed either in action or in flying accidents.

For most of my flying career, the aircraft were more

sophisticated than the homing and approach systems, but people did not appreciate this fact. One of my squadrons was re-equipped with jet aircraft in the pioneer age, when the lack of effective landing aids was exposed for the sham it was. We pioneered flying, approach and landing techniques in jet aircraft, and the civil airlines to a large extent emulated the techniques we evolved. But people were slow on the uptake. On the training agenda, for example, one of the exercises was to deliberately stop one of the engines in the twin-engine Meteor and 'practise re-lighting' that engine. But the re-lighting system was as unreliable as a prostitute. Five minutes after I took command of a Meteor squadron in 1949, one of my pilots turned turtle on the approach, managed to get himself out of the inverted position when fifty feet from the ground, and made a neat belly-landing on the rugby field at Tangmere. His engine wouldn't re-light and on his final approach he decided to overshoot and try again to land. A Meteor on one engine, with the other at full thrust, was uncontrollable. It needed the strength of three gorillas to maintain it in an adequate flying attitude, and one man does not possess the strength of three gorillas. Why deliberately switch off an engine when that action causes you to dice with death? Why not throttle one back, give the other full thrust, and then appreciate that you are now piloting an aircraft which is physically uncontrollable. Any fool knows how to make the movement of re-lighting an engine, but why practise the technique unnecessarily?

Of the hundred or so aircraft types I test-flew – there were no similar dual-instruction types, so your first test flight was also the first solo flight in most of the marques – there are two which I remember with disillusion. The American Mustang Mk 1 was powered with the terrible Allison engine. (Then the Merlin engine was fitted, and the Mustang became the most versatile fighter of the war.) I test-flew three within an hour, and suffered engine failure on every flight. I did manage to land them with their undercarriages down, but swore I would never again test-fly another Mustang Mk 1.

The other was the Swift, a heavy, fast ground-attack, photo-reconnaissance fighter. Like most modern fighters, she required the application of re-heat to get her off the ground; also for landing in case an overshoot became necessary. Re-heat is a process whereby additional kerosene is sucked into the impeller in enormous quantities, exploded and thrust out of the engine efflux. The already considerable amount of kerosene burnt in taking off and flying at low level is about trebled when re-heat is used. On my first approach to the airfield in a Swift, my intention was to overshoot just to get the feel of the aircraft before making my first landing. After the final approach I switched on the all-essential re-heat, only to find to my horror that the system was unserviceable. She was at full throttle in any case, but I had insufficient power, so I immediately raised the undercarriage to reduce drag, and positioned the flaps which were fully down so they were lowered by just fifteen degrees to assist lift. Somehow I managed to gain speed to 170 mph, which was too low for safety on the circuit, gingerly inched her round the circuit at much too low an altitude, put the wheels and flaps down at the last possible moment on the final approach, and landed her fast – but the brakes held without burning themselves out; if they hadn't, I would have finished up in the River Maas about three miles distant.

But there was a simple principle invented by the Royal Flying Corps, one to which I always adhered. If you are involved in a flying accident, but are not too badly injured to be able to fly an aircraft, then it is essential that you take to the air again as soon as possible. After my extremely dangerous interlude in the Swift, I taxied back, climbed into another which was in need of an air test, and took off again. This one remained serviceable, all systems go, and they kept going. After I had landed her, I was master of the Swift. If I had allowed myself time to brood over the might-have-beens, the Swift would have defeated me. As it was, I conquered her. In general, psychologists agree with this philosophy. Military aviation consists of taming your aircraft but, above all, keeping her tamed. I loved my aeroplanes, but I realized very well that if I did not keep them on a tight rein, they could kill me as dead as a coffin nail in seconds. It all amounted to a kind of love/hate relationship such as one might have with a beautiful mistress who is amorous when the mood suits her, but would also be perfectly liable to pour poison into your ear if her mood changed.

Joining No. 66 Squadron was analogous to going down a coal-mine for the first time, living at the coal face for two years, and being uplifted with a degree in coal-mining.

My degree in gold-mining took me another twenty years to attain. The finger that turns the dial rules the air.

> In the last battle,
> Borne down by the flying,
> Where mingles war's rattle
> With groans of the dying.

TRUE ADVENTURE—AVAILABLE IN GRANADA PAPERBACKS

Kenneth Ainslie
Pacific Ordeal   75p ☐

Richard Bach
Stranger to the Ground   £1.25 ☐
Biplane *(illustrated)*   £1.25 ☐
Nothing By Chance *(illustrated)*   £1.25 ☐

Henri Charriere
Papillon   £1.95 ☐
Banco   £1.50 ☐

Emmett Grogan
Ringolevio   £1.95 ☐

Clark Howard
Six Against the Rock   £1.25 ☐

Alfred Lansing
Endurance *(illustrated)*   £1.95 ☐

All these books are available at your local bookshop or newsagent, or can be ordered direct from the publisher. Just tick the titles you want and fill in the form below.

Name _____

Address _____

_____

Write to Granada Cash Sales
PO Box 11, Falmouth, Cornwall TR10 9EN.

Please enclose remittance to the value of the cover price plus:

UK 40p for the first book, 18p for the second book plus 13p per copy for each additional book ordered to a maximum charge of £1.49.

BFPO and Eire 40p for the first book, 18p for the second book plus 13p per copy for the next 7 books, thereafter 7p per book.

Overseas 60p for the first book and 18p for each additional book.

Granada Publishing reserve the right to show new retail prices on covers, which may differ from those previously advertised in the text or elsewhere.

GF3781